The Unstoppable Warrior Woman

THE
UNSTOPPABLE
Warrior
WOMAN

Inspirational Stories of Women who Overcame
the Odds and Chose to Thrive

BERSHAN
SHAW

NEW YORK

LONDON • NASHVILLE • MELBOURNE • VANCOUVER

The Unstoppable Warrior Woman

Inspirational Stories of Women who Overcame the Odds and Chose to Thrive

Published in New York, New York, by Morgan James Publishing. Morgan James is a trademark of Morgan James, LLC. www.MorganJamesPublishing.com

ISBN 9781642799156 paperback
ISBN 9781642799163 eBook
Library of Congress Control Number: 2019958028

Cover Design by:
Chris Treccani
www.3dogcreative.net

Interior Design by:
Christopher Kirk
www.GFSstudio.com

Morgan James is a proud partner of Habitat for Humanity Peninsula and Greater Williamsburg. Partners in building since 2006.

Get involved today! Visit
MorganJamesPublishing.com/giving-back

Dedication

This book is dedicated to my mother who is and was an Unstoppable Warrior Woman. She passed from stage 4 breast cancer but her spirit is still alive. She is the one who pushed me to greatness and never let me give up on my dreams.

Table of Contents

Introduction

This book, *The Unstoppable Warrior Woman*, means the world to me. For so long, I never believed in myself or realized I was unstoppable; I wasn't living in my truth. For so long, I hid from who I really am. For so long, I didn't think I deserved to live out my full potential. It wasn't because I had a horrible childhood, was abused, or was told I wasn't good enough—like so many women. It wasn't because I was unaware of the amazing women out there driving change—I knew many came before me and live now to tell their stories.

I didn't feel worthy simply because little girls are socialized to believe that men run the world. Even if we're not explicitly told this, we inherently learn it through everyday experiences with television, magazines, internet, social media, and personal interactions. We are taught throughout our lives that we can achieve happiness if we marry a successful man. As an eight-year-old girl, I watched examples of the husband working and the wife taking care of the house on shows like *Leave It to Beaver* and *The Brady Bunch*.

Without realizing it, I was being taught that men were powerful and I was less than. I did begin to see women making waves in the world—Oprah Winfrey, Hillary Clinton, Maya Angelou, Margaret Thatcher, and more—but they were exceptions. One day, though, it suddenly clicked for me that I was enough.

The click came when I was diagnosed with stage 4 breast cancer for the second time. I was given three months to live and told that cancer was in my bloodstream and to get my affairs in order—and that's when I woke up. I woke up because I had to get busy living or dying. This was my second chance to really evaluate my life and figure out where I was and where I wanted to be.

I'd married a man I loved and adored, but we didn't have the right tools to stay together. He was dealing with his demons and I was dealing with mine, and we were trying to save each other in a broken way. He was verbally abusive, which made me always feel smaller than I was, but he was successful so I tried to put up with it. On the outside, I appeared to have the perfect life, but did I really? It was all about him, and not my own potential. I had to take care of the home and be available for him, but I didn't get to be available for myself. Many women would have stayed and shut up, but I knew I wanted more and deserved more. Many women would have settled without realizing their potential for greatness.

Why do we women get stuck like this? Our whole lives, we are marketed all the wrong things. We are taught to stay young because it's hard to find a man when you're older. All of the slogans in the beauty and fashion industry are about youth and the exterior of our bodies. But stage 4 cancer is a death sentence if you don't believe in yourself and get to work. When I was diagnosed, it finally clicked in me that my worth wasn't about my looks and beauty. My worth came from my story, my courage, my resilience, and my dedication. So many people out there aren't really living their journey—they're simply existing. I told myself that if I do everything I possibly can, live my dreams, and pass away, at least I gave it my all. But if I survive, I need to keep giving it my all for the rest of my life.

Some people do give up, lose hope, and resign not to fight—because the fight is more than one could ever imagine. But that was not my way, the way of the Unstoppable Warrior Woman. After being told I had stage 4 breast cancer, I went into the hallway and said, "God, if you keep me alive, I will motivate and transform women all over the world. Please just keep me alive and that will show me I'm meant to be here." All of the Unstoppable Warrior Women in this book got busy living, not dying—and they spend most of their time helping other women.

My mother didn't make it after her own battle with stage 4 breast cancer. I wanted to live. I wanted to take her legacy and share it, because she didn't get to. After three years of living after my cancer diagnosis, I knew my time on Earth was meant to be. Another click.

My dad is my hero. He grew up in Gilbert, Louisiana—a very small town with one stoplight. He had eight brothers and sisters and lived in a two-bedroom home. He grew up wanting to escape poverty and have more, but he had to fight for it. Between selling watermelons for years, owning an ice cream truck, and then brick laying, it didn't come easy for him. But he was unstoppable too. I saw my dad struggle and hustle to make ends meet but the one thing that stuck in my mind is that he never gave up. He saw everything as possible. He said, "If you have a will, then it's possible." He always told me the day you die is when you stop thinking it's possible.

When the Huffington Post ran an article calling me "unstoppable," it occurred to me that now is the time for each and every one of us to share our story. Because if you've been through heartache and pain, and come out on top, you're unstoppable too. For every woman who's experienced adversity, challenge, hardship, and fear of showing who she is and living her greatness—this book is about unmuting our voices, speaking up, and telling our truths. This is each woman, one by one, raw and real, sharing how she did it.

This book came about because, as an international motivational speaker and business strategist and coach, I speak to many women from all races, classes, backgrounds, and careers—and it amazes me that today's women are still playing small and afraid to step into their own power. They're not only afraid of failure, but also of appearing too dominant, powerful, or bitchy—while most men are willing to take over and dominate any field they encounter because they think they deserve it. It's mind-blowing that women don't naturally envision themselves as the CEO of a company, but instead in marketing positions, public relations, or as a VP. The men I coach almost always see themselves as a global leader or the CEO of a multimillion-dollar business.

Now is our time. This little gem of a book is one of inspiration and triumph. These are women who took pain, difficulty, and roadblocks and made something new, true, and worthwhile for all. (I'm one of them!) Bravery and creativity are in the DNA of every woman. My dream is for these stories to give you the hope and courage to be an Unstoppable Warrior Woman and push on through your own challenges. So, let's begin with my own story—I'm proud to be unstoppable too.

UNSTOPPABLE
CREATIVE WOMEN AND
How They Shine

"These are women who took pain and difficulty and roadblocks and made something new, made something true, made something that is worthwhile for all. (I'm one of them!) Bravery and creativity is in the DNA of women and everyone of us has it. I urge you to take our words and let them inspire you to do the same in your life."

~Bershan Shaw

Bershan Shaw

Unstoppably dedicated to unstoppable women.
Writer, speaker, motivational business and life coach.

My name is Bershan Shaw and I'm a native Washingtonian. I am forty-five and proud of it. Age is really a number. It's how you feel about yourself. You can be thirty and feel like you're dying, or you can be sixty and feel so alive.

I was born in Washington, DC, and my family quickly moved to the suburbs in Prince George's County, Maryland. One of the wealthiest Black counties in U.S., it showed me the possibilities of wanting more and not stopping until I got it. New York City seemed full of promise for me, so I went to NYU and lived my dream.

I truly believe that you are what you feel and know. My journey with stage 4 breast cancer taught me to take care of myself both physically and mentally—you only have one life, better make the most of it. I used to try to hide my age and pretend I was younger because I wasn't confidant about aging and growing into my next chapter. Now, I have embraced who I am. My next chapter is beautiful because it's all about becoming my true self—open, honest and not afraid to speak up and show up as I never did this my entire life.

My bravest moment was when I first started speaking to a crowd. It was a room full of hundreds of people and I had never told my cancer story before. I was embarrassed and didn't want to be known as the sick girl. I wanted to make it seem like my life was perfect and everything was okay; people didn't know I was going to chemo, getting hooked up to machines with wires hanging down, and in the hospital every other week for tests. I would pray and cry every day to live. That day, October 2011, I shared my truth with the world, and they responded with a line around the corner waiting to speak to me.

Someone in the crowd stood up and chanted, "YOU ARE A WARRIOR!" and then the entire room started to chant "YOU ARE A WARRIOR!" That's when my warrior brand was born and I became America's #1 Warrior Business Coach.

Being a woman hasn't held me back. I am now living my truth and my life isn't over. Yes, we have our obstacles—as a woman, you don't go as far as quickly because we still live in a man's world. There are only twenty-five women CEOs in the Fortune 500 and a smaller amount on boards. But we're making strides, and I'm making changes of my own now. My business has grown with huge success and I speak and coach leaders all around the world. Men and women in Fortune 500 companies listen to me. I'm slowly making changes as the world is slowly making changes too.

It's the best feeling when men don't think you can succeed, but you break down every barrier. They didn't think I would be successful at motivational speaking because most top speakers are men, but I did it. They didn't think I would coach CEOs and leaders. They didn't think this, or they didn't think that, but I pushed through.

I am still on the journey of my dreams, and my dreams are huge. I'm a multi-preneur who believes in being your best self and stepping into your greatness. I also have a successful interior design business and started a cannabis company with an all-women team under Roundtable Wellness, named after the street I grew up on. I believe in transforming your mind, body, and soul. The dream never stops, it only grows—and when I achieve one goal, another one follows.

Besides being an international motivational speaker and business strategist and coach, I also started a URAWARRIOR app and website. The app helps people deal with their mental health and flourish to their full potential in a positive and fun way by motivating the mind, body, and soul. I wanted to launch something that helped people with their mindset and motivation so they could get up and take action to live their best life.

I wish I could have spent more time with my mother and brother, who are no longer on this earth. If I'd known they wouldn't be here today, I would have spent more time with them—but my life was given the way it was supposed to be, and I'm truly grateful for my journey. I live a happy life with great people around me and great things happening. Happiness is a choice. I've seen death knocking at my door and now, I always choose happiness.

My challenge now is dealing with an elderly, fiercely independent dad who is eighty-four going on forty-four. He only wants to date women in their forties! He thinks he's still a spring chicken. Overseeing him is difficult because he wants to do everything on his own, but he is my world and I just have to make it work, like I make everything else work.

I love what I do now! I wish I would have recognized my power and potential at an earlier age so I could have saved more women and helped them see the light earlier, but I am where I'm supposed to be. I choose to live my life with hope because without it you die. I have made so many mistakes in my life and I have failed tremendously in businesses and partnerships but every set-back was my setup for greatness. I am on the journey of living and learning and I take it day by day. From my core, I believe women should support women.

When you have a huge connection with the universe and God, you realize everything happens when it's supposed to. I don't have children and I'm working on that by getting a surrogate, but this is what I would tell my children: You are beautiful. You are enough. The world will try to change you. Don't let it. Don't conform to the world—make the world conform to you!

Natashia Brewer

Shot in a gang shooting.
Healing musician and writer.

Growing up in Washington, DC, I had my share of trials and tribulations. My father left when I was around three years old. He was a loving and quiet man but struggled with alcoholism for as long as I can remember. My mother tried to do her best with my sister and me. She loved life, her children, and the arts—she had the most beautiful voice I've ever heard! Still, growing up I felt so alone. When I was in elementary school, I was touched inappropriately by a family member. I felt like I had no one to turn to, which caused me to withdraw even more.

My mother became addicted to drugs, and at that point I completely lost any bit of normalcy. I was around thirteen at the time, and her drug use lasted until I was eighteen or nineteen. I witnessed firsthand the destruction and devastation of crack cocaine, not only in my house but in my community too. During this dark time, I remember my mom crying to me to help her stop smoking crack—but I didn't know how to help her. This moment haunted me for a very long time.

When my mom was on drugs and my dad was not around, there were times when I didn't have any food and had to either borrow money or eat at a friend's house. Once, our electricity was even turned off. My grandmothers, my godmother and her family, my sisters, and my friends tried to help me, but I struggled for years with issues around self-esteem, body image, abandonment, neglect, and acceptance. No matter who was around me, I felt invisible, unwanted, and alone—I had no solid point of reference for love and didn't recognize the support when it was there. I eventually found myself looking for love and validation from others, mainly men. Looking for love in all the wrong places? That was me.

I became very rebellious in eighth grade—I cut classes, started drinking (not just wine coolers, but vodka and gin), and lost my virginity. By the time I was in ninth grade I moved from house to house. In tenth grade, I added running away from home to my list. I kept looking for someone to show me love and give me attention. Looking back, I realize I thought that sex was love. In 1990, I joined my high school marching band and discovered a newfound hope. The band provided the family atmosphere I'd been searching for. My band members were like my sisters and brothers. Marching band was the one thing that kept my attention, and it's where I developed a musical ear.

My life began a drastic shift on May 12, 1992. I was sitting at a bus stop talking to friends. We typically had band practice every day, but on this particular day practice was canceled. As we sat on a brick wall, a car full of guys pulled up in front of us. They asked us to come to the car, but none of us did. Suddenly, I noticed another car rounding the corner on my left. In a split second, my life changed. It was not just a couple of shots, they opened fire and were shooting like crazy. I stared into the car, seeing the fire coming from the gun barrels—and I couldn't move. My friends ran, but I was stuck. God's angels were shielding me.

As the cars sped away, I finally found myself able to jump down off the wall, but something wasn't right. I looked down and my foot and leg felt numb. I'd been shot. By the time I realized what was going on, I heard the sounds of my friends crying, police sirens, and an ambulance. I limped to a place to sit and my classmate helped me take off my shoe, blood pouring out. As I waited to be put in the ambulance, I stayed strong and never shed one tear. There was something in me that couldn't appear weak or vulnerable; however, when I was taken away, I released the emotions I was holding in.

I'm grateful I was shot in the foot and not someplace else. It was a through and through wound—meaning no surgery was needed to remove the bullet. I stayed in the hospital for three days and had many visitors from my family and my band family showing me love. What I'm ultimately thankful for is that God saved me. I was only sixteen years old and I could have died that day. I began to realize I was alive for a reason and that I had a bigger purpose. I just didn't know how to figure it all out and there was no one to guide me.

After the shooting, I tried to focus more on doing the right thing. On the outside I had it together, but on the inside I was still a mess from all the pain I'd collected during my life. I found myself in a downward spiral. I graduated high school, started working full-time, tried college, and had a few romantic relationships. As time went by, more issues and challenges came my way.

In 1996, I wound up in legal trouble after misappropriating funds from my job, trying to help my man out of a situation as I sought his love and validation. My actions caused me to lose my job and be on probation, all while carrying my first child. So many things swirled through my mind—the disappointment to my family, what would have happened to my child if I went to jail, how I got to this point in my life, awareness of the lesson learned, thankfulness for the outcome.

That same year, my mom was battling lung cancer and her health began to deteriorate. As the year progressed, so did the cancer to every part of her body. She passed in September, five months before my son was born. I didn't want to go on with my life, but I couldn't give up because of my son. He saved me in so many ways. I became grateful for my mom's love and that she was no longer suffering.

During this dark time, God continued to cover me, strengthen me, and guide me. I started writing songs and poems, which led to music production. I began to fight for me more, but I still couldn't completely get it together. Years and years went by, and I wasn't happy. I wasn't fulfilled or complete. It wasn't until I separated from my husband and lost my job in 2017 that I took time to figure things out for me. This was the most difficult time in my life, hands down. I never cried so much. In order to find me, I had to find God and strengthen my relationship with Him. He showed me who I am and who He called me to be. The people I thought would call me didn't. The people I thought would stand by me didn't. God helped me realize He was the one I needed.

I'd been with my husband for twenty-two years, and now he was gone. I'd had my job for twenty years, and now it was gone.

Who was I now without these two things in my life? I was all alone, praying every day, surrendering my life to God, and asking for deliverance from all the things that held me back. God spoke to me and said, "Don't focus on the pain you're going through." He wanted me to focus on the feeling of receiving the love I deserve and the love I will be giving to the world, helping people change their mindsets through His glory. Many days and nights I found myself overwhelmed, bills steadily coming in and my bank account getting lower. He said to trust Him, and that's what I did! I had to be strong for my son and daughter.

What God did in my life was no less than a miracle. He delivered me from everything that had me bound and was hindering my purpose. He delivered me from the fear of loneliness, fear of rejection, searching for love in all the wrong places, and my mommy and daddy issues. I'm no longer caught up in people, what they think of me, and how they can make me whole. God made me whole. I don't fear being by myself. When I am by myself, God is all I need. I don't search for love. God is love. I don't try to please people by sacrificing myself along the way. He strengthened my discernment. God set me free!

I left this stage of my life not only a new person filled with love, but having developed products and services to help others get through their stuck moments. In one year, I created a process called "Finding Life's Love Song," wrote the book *Love Song*, made a *Find Your Life's Love Song* workbook, wrote numerous songs for my business, donated my time and skills toward personalized songs for sick children for the Songs of Love charity, finalized testing of a web app I created, and wrote another book called *Biblical Proportions*. All done by the grace of God. He allows certain things to happen in our lives to free us from what destroys us. Look to Him and trust Him, and He will give you love, peace, clarity, strength, and guidance on your path! Peace and blessings.

Shenetta Malkia Sapp

From bullied to beauty queen.
Suicide survivor coach and inspirer.

We now know there is a strong link between being bullied and attempting suicide, as suggested by recent bullying-related suicides in the US and other countries. I was both raped and bullied, and I had an abusive father. In retrospect, my path to attempted suicide seems obvious.

For every suicide among young people, there are at least 100 suicide attempts. Over fourteen percent of high school students have considered suicide, and almost seven percent have attempted it. This is why I started Empowerment Essence during my reigns as Ms. Baltimore United States 2014 and Ms. Maryland United States 2014. I know you're thinking, wait, what? That's right—even though I was told I was too ugly, my hair was too short, I was not skinny enough, and I needed a nose job—I had dreams of becoming an actress and model as a child, and I strongly felt I would make it.

I kept going through rejection after rejection, wearing my mask and getting through on my own without any proper help. I began a successful acting career and left modeling to help train others on avoiding the traps of the industry. Everyone needs a coach, and helping others stay true to themselves is invaluable. You can get lost in the entertainment industry. If God had allowed me to go further than he did when I was younger, I probably would not still be here to talk about it. I had plans, but God had others—and, my, have they been much better. I sit today reflecting on my years of life and am truly thankful for the opportunity to tell you: YES YOU CAN and YES YOU WILL! There will be obstacles, ups and downs, and times when you say, "This is it." But pause— life does matter. There is always hope for you and you are never alone!

Why did I live and not die? God had plans for me to speak life to you. You can be the outcast, the black sheep, the anything else they called you—but, remember, you can also be your greatest you with help, love, and support. Live for you and live through it all. I survived, and I know you can too. Let's be unstoppable!

As I said, you may face continual challenges. It hasn't always been easy being a woman and working certain aspects of project management and property management. Some men are uncomfortable with my assertiveness and love to challenge my knowledge. But being a woman has also lifted me up through the strengths I found within me: the softness of my love, the determination through pain, and the discovery of my essence of being a caregiver.

Even now, I am not where I see myself in my life dream, but I am well on my way. I have accomplished many goals toward the dream of helping others live and not die by suicide. The dream is to travel the world providing hope and help to those who are considering suicide and those who have attempted and still live. As I too had to learn, I will help others take better care of their mental well-being and not compromise trying to get others to accept them.

Some days I'm happier than others, but every day I find some happiness and fulfillment that gives me more push to keep going. My great challenge is still overcoming and protecting my peace. My desire to walk in love and be love through my interactions with others sometimes stretches me thin. I must remember to protect peace by sometimes staying away or saying no.

I would not change anything about my life other than loving myself earlier! That would have changed so much for me. The best advice I can give is to leave room for God's grace to lead you in all circumstances you may face.

Ann Brown

**From Queens to Africa and back again.
A writer's search.**

*B*orn in the Bronx and bred in Jamaica, Queens, I now live in Queens Village in New York City. I have moved all over the place. While I was attending New York University, I had the elegant address of Fifth Avenue and Twelfth Street, having been placed in a dorm that used to be an area hotel. It spoiled me. I loved living in Manhattan.

After graduation, I moved to Brooklyn with my boyfriend and fell in love with Fort Greene, near downtown. From there, we ventured to LA, which had long been a dream of mine. As a child, I'd visit my father who lived there. I actually almost went to UCLA but chickened out because it was too far from "home." Still, I was in love with the idea of LA, and once we moved, the City of Angels was my new love. I loved the weather and, despite what I'd been told about the shallowness of Hollywood, met some genuine friends! After LA, I stayed a while in Arizona, then Connecticut, then Montreal, and Toronto. Lastly, it was off to Africa, where I did long-term stays in Cape Town, South Africa, Ghana, and Namibia before settling in Cape Verde, off the west coast. Now, I've come full circle, back to my hometown of New York, in Queens. All that living and moving took a while: I'm older than twenty-five!

My boyfriend of more than fifteen years, my first love, started having mental problems. He became paranoid and wanted to leave our home to move out of state. I had the option to stay where I was and continue my career, but I decided to move with him. I wanted to encourage him to get help. Out of state eventually meant out of the country, as he became more and more resistant and I started to fear for him. I thought being with him protected him in some way. It probably enabled him, but it did keep him from being homeless and alone for a little while.

In any case, I wound up traveling the country and the world with him. Ultimately, I had to coerce him into returning to the States to be with his family, who thought they could get him treatment, but I stayed in one of the countries we'd visited. Living alone outside the US gave me time to recover from the trauma of being a caretaker to someone who was mentally ill, and in the process of recovering, I found my inner strength again. I wound up building a life there and marrying someone.

When dealing with someone with a mental illness, you can easily get so caught up in the situation that you lose yourself. Thankfully, staying in Cape Verde helped shake me out of this. It's not that there weren't a lot of adjustments to make living in Cape Verde. Sometimes being a woman there can make you feel like you're living in the 1950s, even though the chauvinism in Cabo Verde isn't nearly as oppressive as in other African nations.

There are women in upper government positions, female executives and entrepreneurs, and more female police officers than I've seen anywhere else.

But there are some very antiquated cultural norms, too. It is, for instance, frowned upon for "married" women (whether legally or just cohabitating) to be seen hanging out in clubs, and the household duties still fall on the woman's shoulders, though the younger generation doesn't adhere as much to these strict gender roles. It sounds more than a little old-fashioned, but even for this solid feminist, having clear responsibilities in a relationship can be refreshing. This is something I would have never, ever said before. What isn't refreshing is that men can have more than one woman without anyone batting an eye, but if a woman dates several men, she's not considered a "good" woman. Thankfully, this, too, is changing, as more young women play the field and abandon the sexist setup.

One thing I enjoyed in Cape Verde is that men aren't afraid to be sensitive. They are extremely affectionate. I have to admit, it did take me a minute to get used to the idea of a man who liked to cuddle and enjoyed being caressed. Being a Black woman in the States, I often found a lot of responsibility placed on my shoulders—from taking on apartment hunting because my boyfriend would steer toward bad neighborhoods to hailing taxis when they wouldn't stop for him. It was often out of necessity and due to racism. These may sound like minute inconveniences, but a lifetime of having to take on tasks due to prejudice is extremely taxing and depressing. In Cape Verde, I could let my defenses down and exhale. Though people often say it's hard to make good friends as an adult, I met people in Cape Verde who became, and remain, some of my closest companions.

Fortunately, in journalism, I didn't find much gender discrimination. Being Black did make a difference, though. I know I was not let into certain white publications because of my race, and the ones I was let into made me feel as if I was being treated as a novelty at times, which was not pleasant.

What I have also come across, especially at women's magazines, is that people like to prove their status. You have to have the right designer clothes, the right haircut, the perfect accessories. Although do I love fashion, I have never been a slave to brands, and would sometimes find myself cut out of the circles of women who followed this lifestyle. In Cape Verde, some people would call me simple, because even there they were particular about looking a certain way. It's not that I'm a sloppy dresser, but I'm also not one to put on my Sunday best for a trip to the post office. I lean toward practical.

Being a woman has lifted me up through the other women I've met and befriended. I'm blessed to know some powerful, determined, helpful women who believe in empowering other women. I hope today that I am also that sort of woman. I can't say I'm happy all the time, but I am content and happy most of the time. I would love to be thinner and richer, but in my life now, I find myself laughing out loud more. One of the things that attracted me to my husband is that I could be silly with him. If I could have a do-over in life, I would have children. When I was younger, I worried about working and making ends meet. I wanted my freedom, to be able to move around at will. I didn't think kids would fit into that lifestyle, but now I think I would have made it work.

I moved back to New York City after nearly eight years living in Africa, and now I am revamping my career. While in West

Africa, I taught business writing to professionals at the Spanish Embassy in Praia, the U.S. Embassy, the Ministry of Justice, Coca-Cola Cabo Verde, and Agência Nacional de Comunicações, among others. I also worked as a freelance writer and an ESL teacher for Cape Verdean professionals. What's funny is that I never fully picked up the local Kriolu language or the official language, Portuguese. My husband still laughs at my attempts to speak Kriolu. Luckily, the English language company I worked for insisted on students speaking "English only" as an intensive program. What made it difficult for me to truly grasp Kriolu was that each island has its own regional variation. Even some of my Cape Verdean friends from the main island of Santiago have difficulty understanding people from the island of Fogo, for example, and some city folk don't understand the dialect of speakers from the countryside.

When my editors found out I was living in Africa, suddenly I was their go-to Africa expert. Mind you, Cape Verde isn't even on the continent. It's a group of ten islands off the coast of Africa. I tried my best to use my writings to show a different Africa—one full of hardworking people, innovative entrepreneurs, beautiful beaches and countrysides, and beautiful people. I even launched a Facebook page called An American In Cape Verde, which became so popular I still maintain it.

I try to dispel the myths about Africa. When I got back to New York, people had so many questions. Even my family, who had seen photos from my time living there, would ask me if there are roads or ice cream there. It's amazing how many people think Africa is still in the Dark Ages, and how many people don't realize how diverse Africa is. I met people from all over the world living in Cape Verde: people from Nigeria, Senegal, Guinea Bissau,

Angola, Germany, Austria, Italy, Spain, France, the UK, and, of course, Portugal, the islands' former colonizer. There is also a huge Chinese presence.

Because there are people from all over the world there, and since everyone from the various islands has a different look, anyone could be Cape Verdean. I was often mistaken for a Cape Verdean from an island called Brava. In fact, my husband thought I was Cape Verdean when he first met me . . . until he spoke to me in Kriolu and I didn't understand. He caught my American accent trying to roll my Rs and then spoke to me in English. We bonded over our love for hip-hop. Our first meeting led to an hour-long discussion on East Coast versus West Coast rap. I, of course, said Biggie was the best MC; he was a Tupac fan.

Here's an interesting fact: There are more Cape Verdeans living in the United States than on all the islands of Cape Verde combined. Cape Verdeans started coming to the States generations ago, initially to work in the fishing industry. I'm challenged to help change some of the world's views about Africa, so I'm going to try my hardest. My husband and I decided to leave because he wanted to see the States and kick off his music career here, and I wanted to spend some time closer to my aging mother. When we left, I made a to-do list of things I wanted to do in my personal and professional life. My challenge now is going through the list and making it all happen, which I am determined to do!

The only major thing I would change about my life is to stop putting the needs of others before mine. I'm working on this and getting better and better at it each day. I learned this from my mother, who does the same thing, and I'm trying to break the cycle. My husband Eder, a singer who goes by the name ELL Cosme, has helped with this. He's always reminding me it's OK to say no, and that I don't have to feel sorry for saying no.

Funny, my dreams keep changing and developing. I'm still dreaming of new ways to make progress toward achieving my goals, and I think that is what makes me unstoppable.

TURNING YOUR PERSONAL VISION INTO
Unstoppable Success

"These are women who, no matter the odds, kept on going until they arrived at mega-success. And even when they arrived, after years of hard work, most of them turned to new challenges and achieved success there. They are unstoppable and teach us the stunning good in front of us if we just keep going."

~Bershan Shaw

Vanessa Bell Calloway

Film star and concert modern dancer.
Married in Hollywood for thirty-two years.

*E*ven though I was born in Toledo, Ohio, raised in Cleveland, and lived in NYC, I now live in LA.

At sixty-three years old, I've had lot of brave moments, but cancer was one of my bravest. Keeping myself motivated by looking forward to the future kept me from becoming depressed. My faith, trusting in God, and believing that things were going to work out fine kept me grounded. I have to be honest because, at times, it took a lot to be brave. I was diagnosed with ductal carcinoma in situ (DCIS), meaning the cells that line the milk ducts of the breast had become cancerous, but not spread into the surrounding breast tissue. It was stage 0, but I still had to do something. I had two lumpectomies, a mastectomy, and breast reconstruction surgery. I chose the flap reconstruction, which means fat from my stomach was used to create my new breast. I was advised it was best to

27

use your own body tissue and I'm so happy I did! It's been eleven years and I love it!

Being a Black woman in a white-male-dominated world in the entertainment industry has had its challenges, too, believe me. The entertainment industry has evolved in the last ten years. I've been blessed, like Viola Davis and Kerry Washington, by starring in *Saints and Sinners* on Bounce TV, now going into our fifth season. I seriously hope young actors understand the privilege they have with such a variety of television shows and streaming services. It wasn't like that when I got started; we didn't have many options. For Black women there was one role, the sidekick of the lead, and everybody auditioned for it. If you were too cute you couldn't get the role of friend of the white girl.

I began my career as a dancer and in the years following *Coming to America*, I appeared in *What's Love Got to Do with It*, *The Inkwell*, *Crimson Tide*, *Daylight*, *Harriet*, and several other movie roles. I've had guest and starring roles on several TV series, including one of my favorites, the prime time drama, *Under One Roof.* Some of my other television roles include *Hawthorne*, *Shameless*, *Black Monday*, and *The Games People Play*.

I've been recognized for my work and received eight nominations for the NAACP Image Award. I won the NAACP Theater Award for my one-woman play, *Letters From Zora*, about the famed renaissance woman Zora Neale Hurston. But, imagine what I and a lot of other women could have done if we'd had a fair playing field back in the '80s when I was in my twenties trying to create content and star in multiple productions. We didn't have many opportunities available to us, especially being Black.

In addition, as women, we still don't get equal pay for the same jobs. There's a lot holding us back. The #MeToo movement is great but I think we also need an ageism movement, especially in Hollywood. Men are rewarded for getting older, but they make women feel like we need to go somewhere and die. We shouldn't mind telling our age, we should be proud. Getting older is a privilege and not a given and we should wear our age like a badge of honor. However, age can play against you. I'm OK with my age, but I'm sure telling my age probably has hurt me in my career. We don't get to celebrate getting older, being strong, bearing children, having and beating cancer or overcoming any adversity. We get penalized for getting older. What am I supposed to look like at sixty-three? Hollywood always wants younger actresses, although the men are old as hell. We need to work too.

Men get away with a lot. Women will stand by a man's side for years and the man will trade her in for someone younger. No one looks young forever. Age with grace and look good for your age. God willing, I hope to look good up through my nineties.

Women are great beings, very detail-oriented and imaginative. We are mothers and wives. We keep our families going, make the house a home, get creative, uplift everyone else, multitask, and make sure everyone has what they need. We are simply AWESOME!

I have not quite succeeded in all of my life's dreams, but I have succeeded in several areas. I have succeeded in being a mother and wife. I always wanted to have two girls. God blessed me with two incredibly talented and beautiful daughters. My dream is to see them as happy, productive, and successful women. They will be thirty and twenty-sixth this year. Although they are not yet married, nor are they mothers, when the time comes, they will be good at it. I share a lot with them, and we're also friends. I accomplished a lot in my career and I'm grateful but I feel I haven't scratched the entire surface yet. I have so much more to accomplish. I'm never giving up!

If I could go back in time, there are some things I'd do differently. I sometimes wonder if having better representatives when I was a young actress would have made a difference in my career. Back in the day, they acted like they did you a favor because you were Black and you should be happy to be in the mix because many people would die to get the job. Now it's somewhat different, although we still have a long way to go. Minorities are finally included in television and film projects. The industry is realizing that depicting the world we live in realistically is very powerful. I'm glad I moved from NYC to California but I'm also glad I had the New York experience. If I'd had an opportunity for a stronger support system when I was younger, that would've been helpful to me.

Most times, I'm just like everyone else, I'm happy. Basically, a lot of the time I'm determined not to be unhappy. Happiness is a choice. We determine what space we are going to live in. I don't have a miserable life. I have a very blessed life but there are moments I feel down. It's my choice how I deal with those days, so I put on my big-girl panties, change my perception, and jump back in after a good cry. I'm a letter-writer—I like to get all of my feelings out, without interruptions, by writing them down. I find this helpful because I have time to think about exactly what I want to say, add things, and then edit my letter if needed. When I send you a letter, believe me, I'm saying exactly what I want to say.

The gift that keeps on giving and makes me happy is the film *Coming to America*. I had such a memorable part in the movie and I'm quoted all the time, my picture is used and people dress up like me for Halloween and even weddings. We completed *Coming to America 2* and I'm excited to see the fans' response because I know it's going to be funny as hell!

My challenge right now is staying in the game artistically. Everything is about young people and technology so staying relevant is important. Staying visible and current is a lot of work, that's the big challenge we all have today. Making sure I age well, mentally and physically. Keeping my weight together, making sure I look and feel good. People see you and that's how they hire you. Staying connected with people. Staying connected with kids, husband—it's challenging because I can get in my own world but have to stop and stay connected to others.

If I could change anything about my life right now it would be my connection with people — making sure that I build a stronger connection with those I love.

The advice I give my daughters is be a blessing in order to be blessed, give of yourself to other people to receive your blessings, listen to your inner voice. If it looks like a duck and sounds like a duck, it's a duck. If you walk into a party or anywhere and something isn't right, turn around and leave. Your inner voice tells you what to do, listen to that voice. It won't lead you wrong. If something scares you, run toward it, not from it. If it seems hard, run toward it. It makes you stronger, smarter, and better and remember you can figure out how to do it anyway.

Final thought: Stay ready to be ready. If you don't like your teeth or whatever it is you don't like, then DO something about it. How you look on Friday is how you will look on Monday. You won't lose 10 pounds over a weekend. So do something about it if YOU don't like it. To survive in Hollywood down through the decades, you've got to be an Unstoppable Warrior.

Michele Hughes

Honored by President Obama.
One of the all-time top-ten successful women in the US.

*I*t's interesting to be a trailblazer. In the mid-1980s, I once sat in the president's office of a New York finance company, situated on Park Avenue, where I worked as one of only a few women. He was a mentor to me. In walked one of the older partners. I felt pretty good about myself when this senior partner said, "I guess congratulations are in order, but I must tell you, I never thought I would see this day." My response to him was, "I know you have a daughter and a granddaughter, and I think you should let them know you work with someone who just broke the glass ceiling." He looked at me and said, "You know, you're right."

We had other women, but we were few and far between. We had to search for our support group. In the '70s, I was a founding member of the International Women's Forum, along with Barbara Walters, Ellie Guggenheim, and others. New York City was where it all started. I came back to San Francisco, got in touch with Cyril Magnin's daughter (founder of I. Magnin), and we founded a chapter on the West Coast. I found out that more women than I could imagine were looking to connect. The organization now has around 7,000 illustrious women from New York, Chicago, Washington DC, and San Francisco. It's been almost fifty years.

I hear some women complain that "you can't get ahead," "the glass ceiling" is a barrier, etc., but things have changed so much. Silicon Valley entrepreneurs I once worked with couldn't have cared less if I was young, old, woman, man, black, or white—all they cared about is whether I could perform at my job. That's where the playing field levels out: performance. No matter what, there will always be obstacles and those things you have to fight for.

I always tell young women not to let a "no" be the reason you give up or feel negative, because in life there are many more "yesses" than "nos." Be self-reliant and believe in yourself. Have self-confidence, believe in who you are and in what you are creating and accomplishing, and be a warrior. When one door closes, five doors open. If you have the attitude that you are a fighter, you will never give up. Always take risks and work hard. That's the great equalizer. So many men tell me they would much rather hire a woman because, "They work so much harder." I do think the bottom line is your performance.

Yes, we're good at working. We all know women tend to be multitaskers—juggling work life and family life is second nature to us. If you can do that, you're pretty much an Olympic athlete. Women also have great insight, intuition, and sensitivity to situations. We're more communicative and talk to each other, talk to our girlfriends and our guy friends—we're a little more willing to show what we're feeling. In the leadership sense, we can be more patient, offer guidance to others, and take the time to coach.

In my case, I did not have kids. I had a husband who was an equal partner, busy with his job and not dependent on me. He was very supportive and wanted me to be the best version of myself without any insecurity over my doing better than him. I was lucky to have a home life and also travel quite a bit—my husband was understanding of that and supported me because I supported him. I didn't have that challenge in a man that many women have, and I could just focus on my work. Another problem women face is making time for ourselves. For me, not having children and the support of my husband gave me time to do things and have a social life without feeling guilty. I feel very lucky.

Eventually I left corporate life and went into real estate development part-time. This might sound strange, but I never knew I had a gift for vision and creating beauty. I bumped into my own talent by accident. People ask children, "What are you going to be when you grow up?" and I never would have guessed I would love making things pretty. In 1993, I was a consultant with Starbucks (when Starbucks was in its major growth stage) and I went to a retreat in Aspen. Someone there introduced me to a property that I ended up buying—it turned out to be a good decision. My husband discovered that I was a risk-taker with a flair for deals, and joined me later on.

Walking away from Starbucks, opening up a new door, and taking a huge leap of faith into the unknown led me to skills I never knew I had. Living in Northern California, I came across many large homes still in the Dark Ages with much room for improvement, allowing me fertile ground to enrich my talent. I'm a Scorpio, I have eight planets in Libra, and my rising sign is Taurus—if you know anything about astrology, Libra is the sign of beauty and harmony and Taurus is all about business. Maybe just a coincidence, but it supported me when I bumped into my new career path.

Wellness has always been a passion of mine since I was in my teens. I've served on a number of boards and attended a number of wellness conventions. I'm a member of the Academy of Anti-Aging, which is becoming more of a vocation than an advocation. I'm currently involved in a startup company that will make CBD oil and cleanly grow hemp. I've been with two startups so far, so this is a huge opportunity for a serial entrepreneur like me.

When I look back to analyze my life and how it can help others, I would say: Always have a dream. Know what you want to accomplish and take action. If you don't take action, nothing will happen. You can think all you want, but if you don't do, you won't accomplish anything. My advice is to always have an action plan that you complete step by step, and to have a contingency plan. I always like to have a "Plan B." If things in my plan don't materialize or work, then I have an alternative approach. But never be afraid to take a risk and dream big.

That's what I did with real estate, building a company from scratch without any real experience in real estate. I had to learn by doing, by creating something and then learning by trial and error. I had a mentor teaching me and we built the company to significant revenues. I wasn't afraid to take an unpopular approach—selling off trophy properties to get out of debt and maintain a good reputation. It takes a lifetime to build a reputation and a minute to lose it.

Since I don't have children, the support of my friends is very important. My female friends think I'm such a Type A workhorse, but they also love my vision and aesthetic. I'm a good listener and my male friends trust and confide in me, I think because I was the only woman for so long in male-dominated situations. Being well-liked by my peers is not an accident—I've aimed to be a good friend and a good leader, and have stayed friends with many people I've worked with.

Sadly, my husband passed away when I was young, so I miss having a relationship with that same kind of friendship and partnership I had in the first half of my life. I'd like to do a bit more traveling—I have a bucket list of at least fifteen places I'd like to visit. I never want to retire, I always want to be working and finding things that challenge me and meet the vision I'm creating. Being a change agent is very important to me.

My unstoppable nature shows in how nothing can deter me. I've had to come up with solutions through difficult situations, such as when many developers walked away from their properties during an economic downturn and I didn't. I never let anyone tell me no—to me, no means go. Never give up. If you tell me no and I want yes, I am going to be unstoppable.

Gloria Mayfield Banks
#1 elite executive national sales director for Mary Kay.

I come from Detroit but now live in Ellicott City, Maryland. I've done well in life but it didn't start off that way. I had to have the courage to leave my first husband after suffering ten years of domestic violence. I was a very successful professional executive with two small children—one and two years old at the time. Breaking that bondage took a ton of courage.

I was very obviously held back in my corporate career at a computer company partially because I'm a woman. I left that arena and started my own company with Mary Kay, Inc. That was one of the best decisions of my life, making me responsible for mentoring ninety-nine percent women. I truly love teaching women how to become more successful in leadership and their life choices. I am continuously uplifted because I work with women whose number-one priority is enriching the lives of other women.

I have succeeded in my life's dream and I believe there's a formula for doing so. I wrote this many years ago: Become successful, powerful, and wealthy by helping others get what they want and become who they've imagined. Speak, teach, and inspire worldwide. As my family grows stronger in love and respect, I can enjoy the journey completely.

Like many women, I wish I had taken it more seriously on how to invest earlier in my life and buy stock in companies long ago. If I had been better at money management, I would have done a better job passing that to my children. That said, I am very happy and joyful. My largest challenge right now is putting too much on my plate. I have created this by working toward my goals but I always have lots of ideas and the confidence to get it done. Time is always an issue. I would love to naturally want to work out. It's still a daily effort to talk myself into it, but it's important and I love the results.

I would also have a larger expectation for success in many areas of my life. I am ambitious and grateful for the energy I have to carry it out, but doubt still creeps in. There are times I ask too many people's opinions and it slows me down from getting the results I want. I would rather move quicker, fall down, and get back up. My stage is small given what I know God has called me to do—but I believe the best thing I can give my children and the women I mentor is the gift of confidence. The love of the Lord and all that comes with it is my ever-present prayer.

Shaun Robinson

**Unstoppably successful,
Unstoppably grateful.**

*L*ike many of us, I faced a new chapter after leaving a job where I worked a very long time. After sixteen years on a very prominent show, I felt that my soul wasn't being fed the way it used to be. It was a high-profile job and I am thankful for the opportunities that came from it, but I wanted to spread my wings and start doing some passion projects. It was scary at first because, in a way, I felt that the job had defined me. Where would I be without this title connected to my name? But as soon as I released who I am with or without the attachment, I was free to embrace my real purpose. My family raised me in the church and I've always had a strong faith that God will provide. He has.

Like every woman, and especially women of color, I've experienced countless situations where you have to work twice as hard to be thought of as half as good. I worked at a place considered

41

by many women to be a "boys club," so women who were very strong and advocates for other women were seen as "threats" to the system. That, at times, was very challenging. You'd see certain people getting ahead because they were a part of that club. Sometimes it felt very isolating and disappointing. Still, in the face of that adversity, I pushed ahead. I believed that the right people would see what I had to offer.

I'm sure that resolve came from growing up in a family of strong women who created a village of comfort and protection. I was taught I could do anything I put my mind to. I also surround myself with an amazing group of girlfriends who always lift me up and are there when I want to vent, remind me of who I am, and show me where I come from. That kept me going, too.

I've always set goals for myself, and I am sure that helped my path, too. In my early 20s, as a reporter and anchor, I dreamed of being on a national talk show. I created one, and then another at a time when there were only one or two such shows. I also wanted to start a foundation where I could help girls, and I am doing that right now. I had the goal of being a producer and currently have a deal with Lifetime to produce a series of movies. I'm always setting big goals for myself. I want to always have an impact on other people's lives, and I believe I am doing that.

If I look at what I would do differently, though, I would have been a little more cautious about the people I let into my life. I want to help everybody—that's both a blessing and a curse. A person has to want help, to want to make their life better, and I probably would have been more discerning about who those people are. Try as we might, we can't help everyone. I'm the type who tries her best to help people, but I'm learning not to take on the weight of the world.

I've also learned happiness is a journey, not a destination. I know now not to base my happiness on one particular thing. I keep a gratitude journal. I write down the smallest positive thing that happened that day—maybe someone helped me carry groceries to the car, someone said I inspired them, I got a text from my mother saying "I love you," or I had a memory of my father. I love butterflies, and every time I see one, I think it's my dad reaching down from heaven just to say hi. I'm thankful I can find those beautiful things in this world. That makes me happy, as opposed to saying, "When X happens, I will be happy." Still, if I could snap my finger for a magical gift, I would have my mother live in the same town as me so I could see her more often.

My current biggest challenge is that I want to help as many girls and young women as possible. Anybody who runs a foundation knows the challenges of raising money and making an impact. Finding organizations and helping them in their mission is probably my biggest focus. But I take my own advice: Don't give up. I give that advice to my many nieces and nephews. Sometimes it's the person who stays focused on a goal who makes it, not always the one with the most "degrees." It's the person who doesn't give up. I think I've been pretty successful in my career because I'm the person who kept at it. If you stay focused, you will see results. Success is about perseverance and believing you can achieve it.

Ruby D. Lathon, PhD
**From doctoral engineer to health coach
to vegan restauranteur.**

I began my journey when I decided to leave my career as an engineer to live a more fulfilling life. I'd earned a master's and PhD in industrial engineering and had a successful career that was gaining momentum. My resume was stellar, I had worked for NASA and one of the top national defense laboratories in the country, and I'd helped start a successful engineering consulting firm. However, after being faced with cancer and winning the battle, I realized I wasn't living my happiest life and I didn't want to continue working as an engineer. I wasn't yet sure what my passion was or what I wanted to do, but I decided to search until I found it. I followed my gut instincts and found that my purpose lay in helping people heal naturally and live their best lives. I switched careers and became a holistic nutritionist and health coach.

Working only for myself and creating a new career from

scratch, with no safety net, has been the bravest thing I've done and my proudest accomplishment. I feel like I won again!

There were many reasons I wanted to change careers. Being a woman in male-dominated fields like engineering and defense was challenging. I've been questioned and challenged by male professors, male colleagues, and even male clients regarding my credentials and abilities—even when my credentials were more than adequate and oftentimes superior to those challenging me. While I've had to work harder to advance, I don't think it's held me back because I was determined to overcome any barriers to reach my goals. When challenged by colleagues and clients, I was always more than prepared and able to shut down their doubts. I focus on opportunities and solutions—so while sexism certainly exists, I always find a way around it with the help of allies, ingenuity, and determination.

The fact is, being a woman drives me to succeed. Knowing other women look up to me as a successful businesswoman drives me even further. I was born with a strong sense of determination that continues to propel me. When I switched careers from engineering to nutrition, women really supported me by being my main patrons and spreading the word about my work, classes, and projects. I'm very close to achieving one of my life's dreams—to be a successful vegan restauranteur with several restaurants. I'm scheduled to open my first vegan restaurant this summer! I'm on my way! I wish, though, that I would have trusted my gut and my instincts sooner. I would have pursued more fun and joy in my life earlier. But, no regrets! I continue to learn how to pursue my dreams.

Every day, I wake up with gratitude and the goal of being happy. I'm living life on my terms and pursuing my passions, and that multiplies my happiness. I've overcome a lot self-doubt, fear, and insecurities that often weighed me down. Fear of failure, though, has stopped or delayed me several times from moving forward with an idea or project. Allowing myself room for failure was freeing and relieved me of unnecessary anxiety. Letting go of that through introspection and meditation helped me get more in tune with myself, which has increased my joy.

I've had role models along the way who helped me grow. My older sister was my first role model; she seemed perfect and did everything right. So many things seemed effortless for her—style, popularity, even athletic ability. She did everything with class. I certainly looked up to her (and still do) and tried to follow in her footsteps. In graduate school, I met a professor who turned out to be another great role model as I transitioned into my first career. She was also an entrepreneur and directed a research lab, and this was inspiring for me.

The challenge I now face is taking more time to relax, have fun, and enjoy life more. Since I work for myself, I find it difficult to take time off and stop working. Another challenge is getting enough help to assist me in reaching goals and trusting people with certain tasks. I know a good team is necessary for expansion, so letting go of perfectionism, while still finding great, is a necessity. I'm happy with my life but I would like to add a husband/life partner to it, which I'm sure is on the way. Having a spouse will make the journey even more fun and bring lots of support and comfort. I don't have children, but I have nieces and a nephew. My advice to them is to be fearless and trust your gut. I advise them not to be afraid to be different, but to embrace uniqueness and do whatever brings the greatest joy.

I am an unstoppable warrior woman because of my determination to succeed and make my dreams come true despite any obstacles. I didn't come from a place of privilege or advantage, yet I've been able to make many of my dreams come true. I'm determined to make all my dreams come true because I deserve it, and I won't stop until I do.

Me'chelle Degree McKenney

CEO of 3rd Degree Solutions.
Owner of Me'chelle Speaks.

I knew in college that I was different from everyone in my circle. We were from various backgrounds and experiences, but we came together by forming a common bond of friendship. I was confident, full of fun yet serious about getting things done, always smiling and laughing, and the one who made suggestions for great collegiate experiences and activities, so almost immediately I was one of the leaders of the group. I didn't think of it as leading, I just didn't want us to miss out on anything. Even when I didn't want to lead, I ended up in charge; it's just who I was.

When I transitioned into the corporate world, my circle grew and somewhat changed in the next chapter of life. My circle of friends now included professional, college-educated women. While we were great friends, I didn't want to be the ringleader. I had so many responsibilities at work that, when I left my office, I only wanted to take the rest of the day off and chill. Fighting fires all day left me tapped out, drained from leading my team on an ever-spinning wheel of high demand and high output. They understood the mechanics of my career, yet they maintained unspoken but clear expectations from me. I was always sought after as the decision-maker for what we did and a planner of logistics for how we would do it, where we went, and even how we would handle life situations that confronted one or all of us. The truth is that I knew that I was always meant to lead even when I didn't want to. I knew that it was in my DNA and, while I thought it was too heavy a load to carry early on in my life, it remained a significant part of who I was.

Still, my humility held me boxed in and I continued to think of leadership as too bourgeois, so I played it down and told myself silently and erroneously that I wasn't an influencer. Through my life experiences and interactions, I learned and realized from the wisdom I received that I didn't have to dumb myself down anymore. Instead, I was influencing and stretching the thought processes of those around me.

I've accomplished a lot in my forty-nine years on this earth. I've had a successful career, but it didn't happen overnight. I had to deal with the realization that I was a Black woman coming into the business world when the technology age was just exploding. I was in my early twenties when the realization smacked me that I had to work harder than my predominantly white male counterparts at the time. My parents raised me to be diverse and open-minded, and I had many friends of the opposite race—but at the end of the day, I was still labeled a Black woman. Even though I was taught those values and morals, I never really experienced the reality of the hurt and harm from prejudice in high school or college. I thought we were all the same, on the same playing field. Then reality hit again.

I was a project manager for a salesforce training company when I experienced what it was like to be a Black female manager in the early '90s. I realized this was my first time experiencing overt racism, sexism, and ageism. I remember being in tears in a hotel room stating, "I am tired of having to prove myself." My mentor looked at me and smiled. She said, "Are you done?" My response to her was, "Yes." She straightforwardly said to me, "Good, now put on your big girl pants and get over it. It's called life. Suck it up, focus, and handle your business." I don't think I will ever forget that moment. I was stunned. I was expecting some theoretical answer. From that point, I have kept it moving. I may get my feelings hurt or get a little wounded, but once I realize that tomorrow will come and I have another opportunity to get it right, it all works out in the end. had many chances to throw in the towel and give up, but I didn't—I used that experience as a constant reminder throughout my career. As an unstoppable warrior woman, just keep going!

My self-confidence has been misunderstood as cockiness. The difference has helped me get through many situations—a real warrior knows their strengths and weaknesses. They get back up no matter the firing squad, and persevere right through the trial. This is what I did because I decided that as a King's kid, success is my inherited legacy. Looking back at the experience of confronting my blackness instilled another level of boldness, honor, and respect for who God created me to be.

At the age of 28, I applied for a management position. I had paid my dues as a project manager. I had aided in the process of landing major accounts and led some of the biggest projects in the company. Some were global projects and many customers requested me by name. I know I met the qualifications and, looking at my counterparts who applied, I was a shoo-in for the position. I interviewed with the director and company president and they were very impressed with my credentials. They knew I could do the job.

After a week of interviews with several other people in the company, I did not get the position. I was told that my time had not come, that I was a great trainer, and I had plenty of time to become a manager. My male counterpart with less experience got the position. Everyone was shocked, even the guy who got it. I was even asked to work with him while he transitioned into his new role. The company president was an older white man. He was smug and I took it personally, feeling like he stabbed me in the chest. He was not going to let me have that job because I was not a part of the "good ol' boys' network." I was devastated. I was in my office trying to figure out what happened and why. I shut down and beame dysfunctional.

An older coworker informed me that I needed to remember the "ancient negro secret." She said, "At the end of the day, you are Black and a female." Again? Yes, I am Black but I decided, from that situation, that I was never going to be defeated and deflated; I grew thick skin. I became that rough-it-and-tough-it girl, doing all the things that the men in my professional world were doing. They were never going to be positioned above me and I was never going to let them impact me that way again. I worked my tail off to achieve incredible success. My dysfunction springboarded me into a place of confidence—with clarity of my blackness and understanding that the company valued and needed my skillsets. I was determined to show them who I was, "that girl, the unstoppable warrior" full of fire, smart and leading the charge. I worked in corporate America for twenty-nine years. It was not always easy. I shattered the glass ceiling and demystified the "angry Black woman syndrome."

Fast forward in time: I am finished working for someone else. I am the CEO and principle of 3rd Degree Solutions. The liberty that comes with the success of working to achieve, set, exceed, and reset is the most refreshing energy in the world! I place myself around dynamic women—high achievers who push, chastise, teach, and even shield me. I am reaching new heights in my professional career, and I hold the responsibility of making the decisions, accepting the results, and working further to achieve more. I am a master networker, and now it is my leadership and skills that charge others to understand the power of their actions, connections, and blueprint to what they desire to achieve. I am working to grow beyond borders, beyond differences into one of the most sought-after agencies in the world.

I was forty-three when I said, "I do." I got married because my career was in a good place and I was ready to share my life with someone. I was committed to what marriage stands for and why God created it. My parents have been married for forty-three years, so I witnessed what a good marriage looks like. Marriage is the hardest thing I've ever done in my entire life. I always heard people say marriage is a lot of work, but I never understood what they meant by that. I honestly had cow-jump-over-the-moon expectations. I thought I would be slinging booty everywhere. The reality was that I had to go through a transition period because I had never lived with anyone before. I was so overwhelmed with this life event that simple things would set me off. I felt paralyzed inside. I realized that when I can't thrive, I feel like I'm drowning above and below the water. My marriage has brought me to a closer relationship with God. I had to go from warring with myself to warring within myself, allowing the Holy Spirit to heal and fortify me internally to be unstoppable. The circumcision of my heart is still taking place. I am working tirelessly to be the woman He designed me to be, His masterpiece. I am His daughter. Once I became renewed and strong, I was able to say, "God, Your will be done in my life."

I went on a sabbatical alone and spent a Christmas in Puerto Rico. I was completely burned out with life. It was there that I determined that I won't wait until I am suffering and struggling to ask for help. The warrior stood up strong in me, and my resolve for life charged forward. I had a prolific encounter with God in Puerto Rico, and I penned a number-1 best seller titled, Get Your H.O.U.S.E. in Order: A Busy Person's Guide to Get Order in Your Life. I got my heart and soul synchronized and recharged. As the waves washed up onto my feet standing on the shore, I saw unlimited possibilities and opportunities. I sought restorative courage, and God blessed me to know that I am enough. I believe. I am charging forward! I am an unstoppable warrior woman!

Natalie Forest, Ph.D.

An advocate for positive change
in her own life, others' lives and the world around her.

*B*eing a woman means there are times when people do not take you seriously or when they make assumptions about what you can and cannot do. This can hold you back and doors won't open. In my case, this was reflected in other women being afraid and unwilling to collaborate. I actually experienced more challenges from other women than from men. I'm also happy to say that when women join together, there's a greater chance of not being held back. I'm a proud member of CEO Space International, the National Association of Professional Women, eWomenNetwork, Women Owned Business Club, the International Women's Leadership Association, and the National Women's Political Caucus—all organizations that help in that goal.

Women are amazing, the way we can multitask, feel, give love, nurture, give birth, and also accomplish our dreams. I love being a woman, and I enjoy having a man open doors for me. This is what I teach my daughter—women have a long history of being the strongest people and the best leaders. We are Pharaohs.

I've succeeded in some of my dreams, but I keep dreaming and challenging myself, so don't know if I will ever accomplish all of them. The dreams I pursued and accomplished are: earning a PhD in history, being a teacher, becoming a mother, being a servant-leader with nonprofit organizations, having my own business with a number of books that help others live happily, having an online TV show after doing radio shows, and being a good daughter and sister.

I believe we are always where we are for a reason . . . to learn. In hindsight, maybe I needed to learn more about being paid appropriately for what I do because I volunteer a lot, but volunteering has its own rewards. I've volunteered as vice president for the board of the Alliance of Women in Media National Capital chapter (AWM-NCAC), in addition to serving in voluntary advisory roles for many other organizations. It comes with happy recognition: in November 2017, I became the proud recipient of the 2016 President Barack Obama Presidential Volunteer Service Award. Happiness comes from within and thus I am always happy. I have challenges and, yet, there is always an inner sense of happiness. I'm happy when creating positive progress as executive director for the Women of Global Change, a premier social impact organization working on positive change across the globe for years.

My biggest challenge right now is figuring out how to move closer to my mother, who still lives in my home country of Germany. Though we see each other often, I realize she's getting older and I need to be closer to her so she's not alone. The other challenge is creating an educational nonprofit to change the way education is done in the US. It's always a challenge to help leaders, corporate teams, and entrepreneurs identify consistencies for their success. I use techniques I've developed to address human capital, leadership, diversity, and change management in business and personal situations, which I believe will cause them increase productivity, teamwork, and retention—resulting in higher profitability, authentic fulfillment, and less stress.

I still need to grow. Perhaps I need to make different investments to ensure sufficient money for my family; perhaps I need to focus on my nonprofit versus helping everyone else with their work. We all need to learn that everyone has an opinion on everything. I always advise those I love to make sure you know why you think what you think. You are amazing, unique, and needed, and this is your life—do the research, evaluate, and make up your own mind without worrying what others say.

I've survived many challenges. On a personal level, I overcame moving to a foreign country and ending an abusive marriage to find hope and love. Today I have a thriving relationship and an amazing daughter. Raising my daughter is both the most challenging and most successful thing I have done. On a professional level, I get to improve lives every day through mentoring. Every day I help at least one person learn or relearn their own value. Through my "Hidden Power of Patterns" process, we've enabled thousands to create their mission in life and find the life they desire. The goal is the realization that everyone can live the life they want, be happy, have success in relationships, and stress as little as possible.

I am unstoppable because I don't give up. I'm on a mission, regardless of how many detours and roadblocks there may be. I continue every day to be fully authentic and in alignment with myself. I don't stop connecting and helping people. I have a stake in the world, and nothing can stop me from leaving it a better place when my time comes.

Chiranda Hunter

From homeless to expert in terrorist financing to assisting entrepreneurs.

My life journey began to make sense when I learned everything I've gone through has not been in vain—and gave myself permission to forgive, heal, and challenge myself to believe things will always work out. I made it through months of sleeping in my car when I didn't have a home, the murder of my closest friend, and the devastating murder of my godson just five months ago. I made it through the day I woke up and realized my body had shut down and I couldn't move; I went to bed one way and woke up another. I made it through my daughter's severe allergic peanut reaction and the stress and anxiety that tried to overwhelm me. I know that God held me up and will complete the work He started. Although being vulnerable in this way is uncomfortable for me, I know that even with all my imperfections I'm perfect for the purpose God has placed in me.

Being a woman hasn't held me back. Through seventeen years in corporate America, I've faced and overcome undeniable challenges when sitting at tables with no one who looked like me. I've been tasked with worst-case scenarios and asked to bring the best solutions in a fraction of the time others had. I had to do more, but everything I learned as a result helped build me. One day a coworker said I was crazy for doing things like raising my hand for projects when I wasn't being paid more for them, and I remember telling her, "They aren't paying me now, but they will have no choice but to later." Now I go in expecting at least twenty percent above the stated pay.

The birth of my daughter was one of the absolute best gifts of my life. Everywhere I look, I see amazing examples of women, starting with my grandmother and my mom—a powerful prayer warrior and vessel of light and love who can make a meal out of nothing. She has always talked to me about being a lady, kind, respectful, and more than a pretty face. Women are overcomers. We are resilient. We are birthers of life, courageous, smart, and filled with compassion, strength, the will to live, and the faith to move mountains.

We help provide solid, lasting, and loving foundations in the home and family. Being a woman has allowed me to connect with other amazing women. Women are diamonds. A diamond is said to be the hardest naturally occurring material on Earth, much rarer than gold and recognized as the only gift that can pass through many generations and look exactly the same for each owner. It means the world to me that I get to raise a Queen, and every day I ask God to help me be the best mom and the best steward over the life God has given me to guide and lead.

I am constantly growing and evolving. I challenge myself

daily to be better. I started to wake up in 2013 and my entire life has shifted from who I thought I would be. When I was younger, my dream was to be a lawyer. I did not become a lawyer. Later in my life, I decided to reinvent myself and became a successful expert certified in money laundering and terrorist financing. At some point, I knew this wasn't the best me God wanted spilling out into the world—and the transition started.

I am currently in a shift and expansion of my life, exciting and scary. Each day I rise and show up to serve, be a bridge and light for others to live out their dreams and goals, make an impact, and be effective and empowering. I assist entrepreneurs in delivering results and pinpointing messages that speak to the needs and solutions of their clients. As a result, their clients receive value as well as profits. Also, very dear to my heart and purpose is being a voice and support for outreach and humanitarianism. I lead an active local outreach community group of more than sixty members and growing.

If I could do things over, I would have focused on entrepreneurship and building wealth much sooner, then used that knowledge to help others do the same. Starting at the age of fourteen, I did hair in my mom's kitchen and had regular clients. This gift came naturally to me without any schooling or training at that age. I stopped doing hair about thirteen years ago and wish I'd had people in my corner when I was younger who would have mentored me, given me direction in business ownership, and showed me how to turn my gifted hands into a business. If I had known better, I would have continued cultivating my talents as a young nineteen-year-old, become a business owner, grown my brand into multiple salons, and showed other stylists how to do it too. I would love the beautiful addition of a husband and family in my life, and also to be in a sustainable place in my business that allows me to both serve my clients and do humanitarian, mission and outreach initiatives without the concerns of money.

Every day I tell my daughter that she is beautiful, I love her, God loves her, her life matters, and to be a good person, operate in integrity, be trustworthy and respectful, laugh as often and as much as she can, speak up, and stand tall in her truth even in the midst of adversity. I tell her that when she knows she is right, to stand on that. I tell her to trust herself and her intuition, love others, have compassion, serve and bless the less fortunate, and live her life in a way that honors her uniqueness, dreams, goals, and what brings her joy. I tell her to put God first in all her ways because she is enough and worthy of every drop of oil that God has placed in her life.

Rev. Dr. Trish Harleston

From an abusive marriage to a brave Pastoral Minister in the Baptist Church. Formed the Harleston Group development agency.

For the last fifteen years, much of my life's work has been in reaching others through ministry through my writing, teaching, preaching, and counseling.

I was born in the small town of Clinton, North Carolina. Clinton was known for pork processing and tobacco harvesting, which partly contributed to my decision to leave in 1979. The options for a professional career other than nursing or education were minimal during the late '70s. Throughout my adult life, I've lived in a total of four cities in three different states. For the past twenty-five years, I've resided in Durham.

Born in 1960, when there were still separate restrooms, public water fountains, and schools for Black people, it was hard to imagine that North Carolina would become an ideal place for young African Americans to thrive in business.

It took a while for me to get there. First, I had to walk away from comfort and security, which took a great deal of courage and bravery. To step out without the assurance of a firm foundation not only requires a great deal of faith in the promises of God, but also confidence in one's personal abilities, resilience, and determination to survive. In 1987, as a young mother and survivor of emotional and physical abuse, I left my home and comforts in Massachusetts with my two small children. My older brother flew up the previous day to ensure the decision to leave wouldn't result in another abusive explosion. We traveled nearly 700 miles in an unreliable vehicle pulling a U-Haul trailer bound for North Carolina.

Escaping a life of pain was a greater motivator than the security of remaining in my current situation. In retrospect, this day changed the trajectory of my life. Not only did the decision open up new opportunities for me, but it removed my children from an inner-city environment that could have resulted in a different outcome for their lives. In our new experience, the support system was strong and, though we still went through some tough times, at least we knew we had a village to help hold us up no matter the challenges.

But there were still more obstacles to overcome. I believe that being a woman has resulted in the delay and sometimes denial for advancement of my pastoral calling in the Baptist Church. Denominational prejudices impact the roles of women in ministerial leadership in all churches, but doors have been opening for women to have influence in the lives of others. Leadership roles have not been as open for women in the Baptist Church, however.

On the other hand, being a woman has afforded me the opportunity to blaze a trail for other women in ministry. As a mentor,

I've been fortunate enough to make seemingly impossible paths reality. Even though opportunities for women in the church have been met with reluctance, many women have been resilient and forged new roads in ministry. The result is an array of women-led ministries in television media, large women-focused events, and literary opportunities to reach the masses both locally and globally.

I believe I'm living God's purpose for my life. Of course, my dream looks somewhat different from God's purpose, but I believe the full manifestation of the dream is still in the very near future. My purpose and my dream have always been to connect and align others to their God-given destiny and to impart wisdom of the Word of God to the lives of others. My dream is not as tangible as many would think, but every day I touch someone's life and inspire them to press forward to be the best the Lord has created them to be.

Like many women, I wish I would have focused more on my personal dreams and pleasing God when I was younger rather than spending years trying to satisfy the whims of others. Now, I try to live my life without regret. Even when perhaps I should have taken another path, I now believe these decisions were incredible life lessons and things would be very different if I had not grown from the experience.

If there's one thing I identify as the thing I wish could have been different, it would be to have known Jesus Christ earlier in my life. Because I didn't trust God, I didn't realize I had the power to overcome much of what I endured. I didn't understand the power that had been promised me, I didn't understand the boldness I had access to, and I didn't know how to tap into the gifts I'm blessed with. Without the realization of the power of God in our lives, we experience a life of trying to "fix" life's challenges on our own, not realizing that we are already victorious. My life truly is the epitome of the grace of God upon the life of someone who made poor choices and bad decisions, but God still caused things to work out in my favor.

Even though I'm not always pleased with how things progress, I'm happy with where I am in life and what the Lord allows to occur through me. For me, happiness and joy are found internally, not through external forces. I'm happy because my life is generally full of the joy experienced through trusting God to lead me and order my steps.

The challenges I face today primarily involve staying committed to the work and the plan when it's not easy to see where I'm headed. It's like walking blindly and trusting that you are exactly where you hoped you would be. I try to live my life poured out, meaning I want to use everything the Lord has placed within me for the good of His people and His glory. The challenge is to always remember that as long as we live our lives in true servanthood, the Lord will provide His goodness and whatever we need to accomplish His goals.

I give my children and grandchildren the same advice: All things are possible through Christ. I remind them to be grateful in all things, speak positivity over their life, and always keep pressing forward—even when it's hard. I have a very close relationship with my children. Although they're aware of the challenges I faced earlier in life, they trust the guidance and counsel I provide them. I'm grateful they can witness my walk with Christ and support the work the Lord has called me to.

Having grown up in poverty and lived as a teenage single mother in an abusive relationship, a divorcée at an early age, and much more, I am certain that I am an overcomer! My favorite line of scripture is, "But by the grace of God I am what I am." I've had various role models in my life during different phases and for different reasons. I admire the drive of Oprah Winfrey, the ministerial commitment of T.D. Jakes, the overcomer spirit of Tyler Perry, and the impact of Joyce Meyer.

I believe I am a warrior woman because I will never stop fighting for what I believe the Lord has for me. I will never stop believing that everything He has planned for me will come to pass. I will never stop pushing other women to reach their greatest ability and operate to their fullest capacity. I will never stop showing others the greatest love we will ever have and greatest friend we will ever need is Jesus!

Carol Pierce

New York City public school assistant principal and writer. Driven to succeed.

I've been driven throughout my life by an intense fear of failure, a strong desire to excel, and an equally strong fear of success. I struggled for everything I accomplished, and even though that's made me angry and resentful, I persevered because I always wanted to be successful.

In elementary school, I was placed in classes for intellectually gifted children. I experienced a lot of anxiety during those years as I tried every day to keep up with children I believed were far smarter than me, yet being thrust into that environment forced me to develop strategies for survival at a very young age. During math, we often reviewed addition, subtraction, multiplication, and division facts by independently completing timed drill sheets. The teachers had us switch papers and correct a classmate's paper. I was afraid if I made too many mistakes I'd face peer ridicule, so

I always chose to "practice" the operation I was already good at, not the one in which I really needed the most practice. I was seven when I took piano lessons. I couldn't translate musical symbols fast enough to keep up the tempo of the piece I was playing, so I assigned a number to each note and rest. Then I'd memorize the numerical pattern, practice it at home on my cardboard keyboard, and play the selection during music class. In this way, I was able to save face.

When I was twelve years old, my family moved from our apartment on Charles Street in New York to a subsidized loft building for artists in the West Village. My parents were excited by the move, eager to be surrounded by writers, singers, musicians, dancers, and other fine artists. My father welcomed having a studio in the building and my mother was delighted that their bedroom was large enough to accommodate a 2,000-pound printing press on wooden beams so she could create her prints at home. But for me, the move to the loft was disastrous. My father strictly followed building management's rules and built walls between our bedrooms that only went three-quarters of the way up to the ceiling. Not only did I lack the privacy I desired, I also could not escape the sounds of my younger brother practicing on his trumpet or the television blasting in the living room at night while I was trying to study.

Shortly after our move to the loft, I realized that I wanted a life very different from that of my parents. I saw them struggle financially—their only source of income coming from the sale of their artwork—and decided when I grew up I was going to have a steady paycheck and a pension. I also knew I wanted to live in an apartment with plaster walls so I could lean against them and relax.

Throughout junior high, I continued to doubt my intellectual abilities and fear ridicule. By this time, my identity and self-worth depended upon being an excellent student. Although I struggled with math and had to reread chapters in novels because I couldn't remember what I'd read, I was petrified of failing and needed to excel with the top students. For me, it was a matter of life and death. If I wasn't an excellent student, my life didn't matter. I was no one. So I persevered, often studying until the early morning hours.

In eighth grade, I was lucky enough to have an excellent English teacher who was also faculty advisor of the school newspaper. She not only taught us how to write news, features, and editorials, but we learned how to proofread galleys, select typefaces, size photographs, and design and layout newspaper pages. We also attended journalism conventions at Columbia University and had opportunities to interface with other student journalists and take seminars on newspaper writing and publishing. I enjoyed interviewing, collecting facts for my stories, and writing them. Eventually, my teacher appointed me editor of the school newspaper, and in eighth grade, I decided I was going to become a Pulitzer Prize–winning journalist. Being a stellar student became even more important, and in later years I spent summers working on community newspapers, had an internship with Village Voice, and worked part-time as a newsroom assistant at Newsday.

In ninth grade, I was traumatized when I didn't pass the entrance exam to Stuyvesant High School, a school for gifted children. I remember the day my junior high school principal announced over the loudspeaker the names of the students who had passed the test and invited them to her office. I was sitting in science class on a Friday afternoon, and all my friends ran out of the room when they heard their names. I sat in the classroom with two other students, and my science teacher asked, "What happened, Carol?" I had no answer. I didn't think it was possible to feel any worse about myself than I already did, but it happened. I felt as if I was ripped away from a cadre of students with whom I identified, and in doing this, I had lost a part of myself.

At sixteen, overwhelmed by enormous levels of anxiety, anger, and depression, I began to see a psychiatrist. My family believed going to a psychiatrist meant you were crazy, so now I was scared that I might also be crazy, in addition to everything else. I begged the doctor to test me because I thought there was something wrong with my brain. She repeatedly assured me my concern was absurd but agreed to have a psychologist administer a battery of tests. I learned that my intelligence was well above average and that I was very creative. My verbal scores were much higher than the performance ones, which suggested a learning disability. Further review of the performance subtest scores and additional testing revealed that I had a spatial perceptual problem.

The tests confirmed for me that I was different. I identified with the label as if I were Hester Prynne doomed to wear her scarlet letter A. Although I was angry that everything was a struggle and I had no one to help me, I couldn't stop because I had to be successful. I was hospitalized twice during high school for depression and when I finally graduated, third in my class of 627 students, I was devastated. There was no recognition for being third. I didn't receive a medal to wear around my neck, and I wasn't invited to make a speech. I was only number three.

I decided I wasn't going to take the SATs because I feared not doing well, so I only applied to colleges that didn't require them. I attended a private liberal arts college in Massachusetts where student projects replace formal classroom exams and extensive narrative evaluations substitute letter grades. Ironically, I realized I needed the structure of a traditional college. I had developed a block and was unable to complete any written work for my classes or for the school newspaper. I struggled for two years and was finally forced to withdraw. Riddled with anxiety and angry that I had to withdraw from college, I used the proofreading and layout skills I learned in eighth grade to secure a job as a production assistant with a medical textbook publishing company. Within a short time, I was promoted to production editor, and even though I was well-liked and respected for being a conscientious worker, I resented the two or three years I was there because I wanted to be back in college.

Eventually, I transferred to Hunter College and graduated. I was still focused on becoming a journalist even though writing was an arduous task. During those years, I struggled to read and study, and writing papers was exhausting. I got caught up in a vicious cycle of staying up all night and fighting against the block, trying to squeeze out a few words and facing exhaustion and lactic-acid buildup in my muscles when I finished. Whenever this happened, I was forced to cut classes the next day because I needed to sleep.

When I graduated from Hunter, I realized writing under pressure was impossible and that I would have to give up being a journalist, the career I had focused on since eighth grade. I became very depressed. I worked at different jobs but didn't feel satisfied without a real career. I desperately needed to identify with a profession. Then I had an epiphany: I could become an educator and teach students with learning disabilities. I enrolled at Hunter again and took the required courses in teaching reading and mathematics—enough to obtain a provisional teaching certificate—and began teaching the following September. I finally found something

I was good at, enjoyed doing, and could make my career!

I recently retired from twenty-six years with the New York City Department of Education. I was a teacher for ten years, educating students with mental retardation, learning disabilities, and in regular education classes. I obtained a second master's degree in administration and supervision and worked as an assistant principal for sixteen years. Throughout my career, I received awards for excellence in teaching, and I was well-liked and respected by the students, parents, teachers, and fellow administrators with whom I worked.

As I think back on my life and the many obstacles I faced, I only wish I'd known then that everything was going to work out. I've come to see that because of my determination and drive to succeed, I compensated for my difficulties, overcame many obstacles, and achieved the success I so desired. I am finally happy. I own a beautiful apartment in Manhattan and am in love with my partner of many years. I've started to write short stories and still struggle with blocks, but I'm lucky to have the support and wisdom of a wonderful writing coach. To date, I haven't had any stories published, but I am determined to get there. For me, I won't be a "real writer" until I'm published. I keep on working and going until I succeed. It's worked before!

Nicole S. Mason
Giving up is not an option.

I grew up in what is now called Capitol Hill. My grandmother owned one of two dry cleaners in the neighborhood. I was exposed to business all my life and saw firsthand what women supporting women looks like—the power in it and the results. I'm proud to be from Washington, DC. I'm an attorney, entrepreneur, leadership coach, diversity and inclusion expert, bestselling author, wife, mother, and preacher, but there was an arduous journey to become the woman I am today! I pray my story will impact your life and move you into action!

My toughest moment was moving forward with my life after losing my mother and grandmother in the same month, seventeen days apart. I was an only child and my immediate family consisted solely of my mom and grandmother. Although my father was instrumental in my life and I was a daddy's girl, he'd passed away about eight years prior. Learning to live without the support, guidance, love, and wisdom from the two most important women in my life was very scary.

Let's face it, the entire world system is designed to hold women back. This is one of the reasons gender equality is a United Nations focus area. I was always told I could do and be whatever I wanted to be in life. My father was adamant that I should never let anyone put me in a box! If you ask me now whether being a Black woman and everything associated with it has impacted me, I would certainly have a different response than I did as a child. But I love being a woman! I grew up seeing women supporting one another so it has been my life's mission to do likewise. I remember very vividly how my grandmother and her friends borrowed an egg and a stick of butter from each other. When one made a cake or a dish, she shared it with another woman, so they all had something to eat for their families.

Today I approach my ministry and the women I'm honored and privileged to serve in that same spirit. Serving as a leader in various capacities, I've been a coach, mentor, and example to women in ministry. I'm also a leader in the marketplace, serving as the first African American female senior leader in my current position. I've been a trailblazer in my organization, helping to organize and execute the first Diversity and Inclusion Summit and receiving the organization's highest award. I've also received numerous awards for my work with women, including the Maryland Governor's Citation in 2018.

I succeeded in my life's dream of becoming an attorney. I wanted to be an attorney since I was eight years old. I loved watching Perry Mason. I was intrigued by Mason's performance in the courtroom—especially his rapid-succession witness questioning on the stand at the very end, culminating in the witness's confession in an exasperated tone. As I entered a room full of first-year law students, I could literally hear the faint gasps for air as all eyes peered down on me in the front of the auditorium. I was five months' pregnant, and some of the students looked at me like I was crazy. What separated me from the other students in that room and what they couldn't see was the fire of determination and fortitude burning ablaze from within me.

My first son was born while I was a sophomore in college, and I was determined to finish. I took him to school with me when I had to—so much so that he became popular on campus. When I walked across the stage in Howard University's Burr Gymnasium with my three-year-old by my side, my classmates and the audience went wild! He started waving and smiling. It was a moment indelibly inscribed in my mind and heart! Anything is possible if you believe you can do it and put the hard work in to make it happen. These moments are what I like to call "faith files" and "holy highlights"—those times you didn't think you would make it but looking back on the situation, you understand God's hand was upon you. It's these moments that give us the strength and fortitude to keep going, especially when we want to give up. It's always good to pull on the strength of the memory and not just what felt like defeat at the time.

When you embrace every part of yourself—the good, the bad, and the ugly—no one can stop you. When you come to a place of authenticity and self-love and show up as great unapologetically you, you send out a vibration in the earth that puts others on notice that you are unstoppable. You won't back down from challenges and setbacks. In fact, you welcome challenges because you know, understand, and embrace that you have everything within you to conquer them.

Of course, my dream has many tentacles to it, and I continue to unpack those aspects of my dream. I've always loved to write and have been recognized for my writing with awards such as the 2018 50 Great Writers You Should Be Reading and 2019 Indie Author Legacy awards. If I could start again, I would convince my grandmother to let me take over the family dry-cleaning business and grow it into a franchise. Otherwise, life is good. I always advise my children: go after your dreams!

Shareka Lashell Robinson
Determined to close technology's gender gap.

*T*he meaning behind the name "Shareka" is unknown; it was given to me by my godmother, Selina. A search on the internet states: "You are spiritually intense and can sting or charm. Your name brings love and new starts into life and attracts money. In business, you are the creator and promoter of original ideas and usually enjoy considerable financial success. You are bold, independent, inquisitive, and interested in research. You know what you want and why you want it. You desire to inspire and lead, to control others' affairs. You are giving, courageous and bold, action oriented, energetic, and strong willed. You want to make a difference in the world, and this attitude often attracts you to cultural interests, politics, social issues, and the cultivation of your creative talents." I'd honestly have to say that there is a lot of truth to that!

I grew up in Southeast Washington, D.C. and in various cities in Prince George's County, Maryland. My mom was sixteen and my dad seventeen when I was born, resulting in my mom not finishing high school. My dad joined the Army right after his high school graduation while my mom struggled to get her GED. Despite my mother not completing high school, they were both hardworking. My mom became a housekeeper and my dad worked in the transportation industry after serving four years in the Army. While my Dad served his time in the military, we lived in Fort Carson, Colorado. I was an only child for seven years until 1990 when my sister Tymeka was born. I remember the day my mom and dad came home with her. She was so pale in color that I thought, "Where did this pale baby come from?" A few months before Tymeka was born, we had moved from Washington, D.C. to Temple Hills, Maryland, where I attended Hillcrest Height Elementary School. Many days my dad would drive me to school because the walk was a bit far from where we lived. We'd have conversations about everything—school, life, even politics.

During this time Bill Clinton was running for president; my dad would listen to the election updates on the radio along with a little Frankie Beverly and Maze. My dad was very strict and big on education. He would always tell me to bring all of my schoolbooks home even if I didn't have homework. By the time I was in my first year of middle school, my sister Kanisha was born. I attended Benjamin Stoddert Middle School and I didn't like it at all. A lot of the kids who attended this school were mean, disrespectful, and would often tease me because I was dark, quiet, awkward, and nerdy. This environment was unfamiliar to me, and I didn't know how to handle myself or react to such behavior. Many days I would come home from school upset. I would talk to my parents about it and they would always say, "Let them talk, as long as they don't put their hands on you!" and my dad would say, "I'm black too, so!" We'd visit my paternal grandparents at their home in Capitol Heights. Often my grandfather would come by to pick me up and we'd go for a ride to the local corner store or even down to the Capitol Cab lot in Washington, DC, where he worked.

In 1994, my grandparents purchased a new home and we moved into their old home in Capitol Heights. I transferred to Andrew Jackson Middle School, which I absolutely loved. I learned a lot and met new people, some of whom are still my close friends. During my last year of middle school in 1996, my twin brothers, Tyrone and Tyrome, were born.

My mom had four children within a six-year period. As I mentioned, she was a housekeeper and was always working. As the oldest child, the responsibility was left to me to take care of my siblings when my mother and father weren't home. To me, that seemed far too often; there were a lot of things that I missed out on because I was stuck home babysitting my siblings.

As the years passed, my parents' relationship declined. By the time I was going into my sophomore year in high school, they were no longer together. I remember my mother packed us up one day and we moved to Oxon Hill, Maryland. It was not an ideal neighborhood, but I know now that it is what she could afford, with five children. All I knew was that my mother was unhappy; she said, "I'm going to need your help with the kids." I didn't know what had transpired or what made her leave so abruptly, and I didn't ask her why. I later found out that my dad had been cheating with the mother of a girl who went to high school with me. Apparently, her mom and my dad went on a date to a party and a picture was taken. The girl brought the picture to school and showed it to other students. One of the students happened to be a good friend and, of course, he couldn't hold it in! He immediately informed me about the photo, and I went home and told my mother. I had my friend find out where the girl lived, and my mother and I went to her house to verify the information. When we arrived, we saw my dad's car parked in front of their house, and that was the end of my mother's back-and-forth, unstable relationship.

By the time I was in my senior year of high school we were living in Suitland, Maryland. Just like Oxon Hill, it was not one of the best places to live, but guess what? You are not where you're from. That is something I remember my dad saying on multiple occasions and that still resonates with me today. I graduated from high school in 2001 and I didn't exactly know what I wanted to do or be, nor did my parents have money saved for me to go to college. However, they both encouraged and supported whatever I'd decide to do. Although I'd attended one of the magnet high schools and had well-above-average grades, I had never taken the SATs. But I had an interest in computers, which I discovered at an early age. I could always be found saving whatever I typed to a 3.5-inch floppy disk on an old, dinosaur of a desktop that my dad got me. To this day, I have no idea where he got it from or how he paid for it. When we would go visit my grandparents, I would rush to my room to get my floppy disk before leaving home just so I could use my grandmother's computer to open whatever I typed up at home. I thought it was cool!

Two months after I graduated high school and two months prior to 9/11, I joined the Maryland Army National Guard. My parents were very supportive of my decision; both had to sign because I was just seventeen. My dad asked many times, "Are you sure this is what you want to do?" I knew that by joining the military, it would be my "foot in the door" to whatever I decided to do afterwards. I also knew that my mother still needed my help with my siblings. When it was time for me to pick a career and school at the in-processing station, I chose the career with the shortest timeline, just so I could come back home to help my mother and possibly get a job. After I completed all of my required training, I came back home, started working as a data entry clerk for the Department of Education and eventually enrolled in college.

For many years I had a lot of resentment, anger, disappointment, and feelings of abandonment in my heart for my father. I had anger towards him for my siblings as well because I saw how the choices he made affected them. I wanted to protect them, not only because I loved them, but because I wanted them to be the best at whatever they chose to do! Most important, I didn't want the influence of the streets and society to be greater on them than the influence they had at home. Eventually my father began a relationship with another woman and had another child; we were all devastated! I was angry. Although I put on a smile, I wasn't smiling! I'm not saying he didn't take care of his responsibilities as a father, but I felt like some of the decisions he made weren't the best and were absolutely selfish. A lot of the choices he made directly affected my siblings and were the cause of a lot of their bad behavior. Years would go by and my anger would build and build. After an incident that took place between my brother Tyrone and my dad's girlfriend, my dad came over to my house and we had a conversation. I told him exactly how I felt about everything. We talked for hours about life, respect, love, anger, decisions, and guilt—everything!

A few months later my brother Tyrone graduated from high school. Less than a week after that, my father passed away suddenly, at age forty-seven, from a massive heart attack. After his death, my relationship with God suffered to a point where it was pretty much nonexistent. I was angry at Him, too. I didn't under-stand why my dad was taken away so young and without warning. I felt like we had no time to prepare although in reality there isn't a way to prepare for death. I took some time off from work, went to therapy, and it helped a lot.

In May 2015, almost a year after my father passed, during a routine check, the doctor discovered an 8.5-centimeter mass on my right kidney. A nephrologist diagnosed it as cancer before even conducting a biopsy. I didn't believe it and wanted to get a second opinion. After I left the office, I immediately began to cry and question God, yet again! A few days later, I contacted Johns Hopkins and was scheduled an appointment on a Tuesday with a surgeon. After my appointment I was instructed to send a copy of the radiologist's report. On Friday of the same week, Hopkins called and stated that I was scheduled for surgery on Monday. The cancer was stage 3 renal cell carcinoma, and they were worried about it spreading to other organs. The cancer was outside of the kidney in the main blood vessel as well in the tissue directly sur-rounding the kidney.

I underwent surgery to remove my right kidney and, by the grace of God, I did not need chemotherapy or radiation treatment. Immediately following the surgery, I had to return to Hopkins every ninety days to participate in imaging studies to confirm that the cancer had not returned as research states that it could within the first three years to another organ, but I am well, freeing me up to do what I love.

My passion for technology and helping girls resulted in the birth of She.Loves.STEM, Inc. She.Loves.STEM. Inc. is a non-profit organization dedicated to inspiring the next generation of female STEM professionals (those interested in science, technology, engineering, and mathematics). She.Loves.STEM is a direct response to the major gender gap that I've personally witnessed in the technology industry. I've worked in the industry for over fifteen years and I've always felt alone. I've held many technical positions in which I was the only one or one of just two females. With She.Loves.STEM, our mission is to provide programs that will inspire, motivate, increase, and foster STEM interest for girls in underserved communities because I am a girl from an underserved community.

ßI am a girl that had and still has an interest in all things STEM and I want to be a part of the global movement to increase the amount of unstoppable women in STEM!

Mrs. Sandy Gooch
How going Goochable made me unstoppable.

*I*t all began after suffering a life-threatening reaction to tetracycline and a combination of commonly used food additives. I began a search to find out what was good for my body and what wasn't. Luckily, my dad was a research biologist and chemist; after a long process of elimination, we concluded that the chemicals and additives in foods were hurting my body. I started educating myself by reading every book and article I could find on food, and keeping up with the Food Marketing Institute, which is a good source of information on ingredients found in (and not in) various foods. This led me to the idea of a market that focuses on what we were putting into our bodies.

I had very little money, I didn't have contacts in the industry, and I had to create the infrastructure for the country's first natural products supermarket. When I began my venture in 1977, there was only one other woman owner in the nation in the supermarket industry: it was an entirely male-dominated business. Communication was a challenge. People treated me with skepticism. During that era, women were not commonly accepted in upper management or ownership positions. Many thought I would fail and told me so at the beginning.

When I was invited to attend and speak at a marketing conference, I looked around and realized there were three women in attendance: me and two assistants. Before the event began, I was in the conference room with all these CEOs in blue suits having coffee. One man handed me his empty coffee cup and said, "Dear, would you mind filling this up?"

I took the man's cup and refilled it. I walked back over to him, held out my hand, and said, "Sir, allow me to introduce myself. I'm Sandy Gooch and I'm doing the first presentation." He was speechless. Sometimes I caught looks from people at conventions who were certain I'd never achieve my goal, but I was never harassed like the women whose stories have been shared by the #MeToo movement.

When I tried to open my first store, I couldn't even get a loan. Banks were reluctant to offer financing because there was nothing to compare it to, which prevented them from making an accurate projection on its likely success. It was frustrating. I put my own money into the first store. The second store was a limited investment partnership with a few friends. The third store was built on cash flow because the first two were doing so well. Finally, by store four, I was able to secure a bank loan.

As it turned out, I was the first woman to develop a chain of supermarkets in the United States. Over the next sixteen years, I expanded the operation, opened larger stores, and developed a $90 million-per-year business. Spread across the greater Los

Angeles area, my seven markets adhered to strict requirements for freshness and quality. I was devoted to providing a large selection of the finest products available without harmful chemical additives, preservative agents, artificial flavorings, artificial colorings, artificial sweeteners, refined white sugar, refined white flour, caffeine, chocolate, hydrogenated oil, isolated synthetic MSG, irradiation, bovine growth hormones, or GMOs using recombinant DNA technology.

It was difficult to find actual goods to carry in the first store because we had such a rigorous screening process. I would drive for miles and miles to find the right purveyors of goods; I drove to farms to make sure they really were organic. Farmers would bring produce in trucks or the trunk of their cars, or I would go to a downtown produce market. In the 1970s, people were not as focused on organic farming methods and certification as they are today.

I was a stickler for quality: If you wanted to be in my stores, you had to follow my guidelines, maybe make some changes, get rid of the sugar. When the brands did that, success followed. The "Goochable" standards to which I held my markets helped set natural product standards throughout the United States and other countries as well.

We trained employees to teach customers how to cook a variety of foods. We provided free samples and recipes. A full-time nutritionist was available for nutritional counseling. Store tours for schools and other organizations, lectures, and seminars were just a few of the many ways we introduced wholesome menus to the public. In return, they embraced us.

Due to my positive experience of being a woman, I have found other women from various walks of life who became my comrades and confidantes. Networking is essential, and I have found many women facing similar challenges in different professions. I formed many meaningful friendships in various networking organizations as we talked and solved problems together.

My dream was to allow people to have access to food that would bring them health, not illness. I was overjoyed with the success of Mrs. Gooch's. When my seven markets were acquired by Whole Foods, it was sad to say goodbye to my baby and our 830 employees. It was over a year before I could even bring myself to go into a Whole Foods.

Then I started designing, building, and refurbishing estate homes that, to the degree possible, incorporate pro-environmental features. So far, my fifteen successful real estate ventures have out-performed market trends. Among the factors we consider are energy efficiency; water purification and conservation; colorful, engaging, and protective landscaping; and the use of natural building materials rather than synthetic.

I'm a former schoolteacher and master teacher for university students obtaining teaching credentials. As a lifetime educator, I continue to inform the public about the significance of the interrelationship between sustainable environmental practices and the long-term health and viability of our planet and humankind.

I have lectured to many groups and organizations about healthy lifestyles and the challenges that women face in business. I wrote a book called If You Love Me, Don't Feed Me Junk! (1983). I've also been a member and served on the board of the southern California regional chapter of the International Women's Forum (IWF), a worldwide organization of preeminent women of achievement. The organization's goal is to assist women in obtaining new and greater leadership roles in every sphere. It encourages women leaders to forge links across professional, geographical, and cultural boundaries to strengthen prospects for women everywhere.

If I had to make a change, over the course of my career, I would have paid closer attention to the people I hired. I would have investigated backgrounds more thoroughly and thoughtfully. I hope I would have found a way–like so many other women–not to feel guilty about working so hard, so long, and having to hire a babysitter so much. My daughter says she never felt anything but love, and that makes me happy.

I consider myself to be someone who looks on the bright side of life. Right now, my biggest challenge is managing my time and energy to be able to do all the things I would like to do to give back to society. If I had it to do over again, I would make my life simpler and less complicated. I advise my children and grandchildren to do the best they can do and be the best person they can be in all endeavors. I encourage them to increase their skill sets with open minds. In general, I advise them to always be open to new experiences, opportunities, and friends throughout their lives.

People have listened over time. As an early spokesperson for the natural food industry, I've been featured in numerous publications such as TIME Magazine, The Wall Street Journal, New York Times, Chicago Tribune, Denver Post, Los Angeles Times, Los Angeles Magazine, Beverly Hills Courier, Beverly Hills 213, Natural Foods Merchandiser, and Delicious Magazine.

I served on the Los Angeles County Board of Supervisors' Task Force on Nutrition and Behavior, where I helped amass research information on diet and behavior patterns. I was commended by the mayor for studying the effect that providing nutrient-dense foods in penal institutions had on recidivism. I launched the Healthy School Meals Program, geared towards educating high school students, food service directors, and school administrators about diet and nutrition.

I was on USC's Entrepreneur Program's Advisory Council and have been on the Women's Leadership Board at Harvard University's John F. Kennedy School of Government for more than twenty years. The Women's Leadership Board is an international group of over 100 women using their influence and resources to empower, develop, and recognize women as leaders, and encourage and support public policy positions that have a critical impact on women worldwide.

Over the years, I've devoted tremendous time and energy to fundraising for various charitable projects and organizations, including the Haven House shelter for women and children, the Weizmann Institute of Science and Rambam Hospital (both in Israel), and the Community Alliance for Family Farmers. I was cochair of Natural Medicine Now, which was primarily responsible for the passage of Senate Bill 907 that gave licensure to Naturopathic Physicians in the State of California in the fall of 2003.

My work toward making my dreams come true has been recognized with several awards, including the 1992 Entrepreneur of the Year from Inc. Magazine and Ernst & Young; consecutive awards in 1990, 1991, and 1992 for Retailer of the Year from the Los Angeles Business Journal and National Association of Women Business Owners (NAWBO); one of 1991's National Organization of Women's (NOW) Women of the Year; the Women of Achievement Award from Beverly Hills Women's Network in 1992; Retailer of the Year from Whole Foods Magazine and the Women of Vision Award from Valley Presbyterian Hospital in 1993; numerous awards throughout the years for innovative advertising from Food Marketing Institute (FMI); and one of the Top 50 Women Business Owners in the United States from the National Foundation of Women Business Owners (NFWBO) in 1993. I have also been featured in Working Woman Magazine. In 1994, I was inducted into the John Muir Alumni Hall of Fame; other recipients of this award include Jackie Robinson and Dr. Willard Goodwin, the first doctor to perform a kidney transplant. In 2003, I was the only woman to be chosen among the Fifty Visionary Leaders Who Transformed Food Retailing by Supermarket News.

A Sandy Gooch Day was declared in Beverly Hills, and Whole Foods Market gave me an achievement award entitled "You Have Changed the World" and held an event to celebrate my achievements in the natural foods business and my community building efforts. I was selected as one of the Leading Women Entrepreneurs of the World for 2001. To receive this most prestigious global award, I went to Madrid, Spain, for the fifth annual Millennial Gala. As you see, it can pay to be unstoppable.

Ari Squires

From felon to filmmaker, internet host, and motivational speaker.

*B*efore being a speaker, business coach, filmmaker, and motivator, I was a felon. I was a young woman with low self-esteem who made a lot of bad decisions that got me in a lot of trouble. I was attracted to the fast life and got caught up in the streets. I was so lost, even though I was raised in a good, upper-middle-class home. I wanted to prove that I could live up to who people thought I "should" be. That's who I was for a long time, until I met someone who saw the real me and helped me create a more fulfilled life. I married him!

Being a woman has held me back in situations where I was in leadership. Men sometimes tend to not want to take direction or orders from women. It seems so easy and expected for men to take a leadership role, but not so easily is that respect and consideration given to women. Because this is often the case, I was not given

95

opportunities that I deserved.

Like many women who watched my film, *No More Chains* (2017), I see myself in all the stories. One in particular is about a young lady who had her own dreams as a teenager but was held back by the lack of support from her parents who wanted her to play it safe. You see, you can be held back because you are a woman, but you can also be held back because you are a daughter. The dream-killer in my home was my mother. It wasn't her fault. She only knew what she knew. She encouraged me to go to school, get a degree, and work as an employee, but deep down inside I wanted to be an employer.

This story in the film resonated with me because our chains can be held by the people who love us the most. That's a hard one to break. Both of our stories prove that we have to stand in who we are and go for what we know is best for us, even when it may hurt someone else. We still have to follow our own hearts. When you hear the word "chains," you automatically think bondage or being held captive with limited mobility. It easily gets your attention because almost every woman has felt stuck at least once in their lives. We feel so bound up, we can't imagine being able to kick or claw our way out.

I have a presentation titled "Release the Chains" that I've been doing at women's events for the past few years where I walk out with chains wrapped around my shoulders and arms, and I talk about the four F's to Freedom. I provide an experience to show women how to release their chains of Fear, Focus, Failures, and Forward Movement. I remind women that we must fight for our dreams and move forward past our traumatic experiences. "Release the Chains" led to my *No More Chains* book anthology in which women share their own personal "Freedom" stories; the similarly titled documentary was birthed from there.

For many years I tried to find employment with a felony on my record. I couldn't find a good job anywhere. No one would hire me. This actually turned out to be a good thing because entrepreneurship was always my calling. I said to myself, "Well, since no one wants to give me a job even with my college degree, I will create jobs and be my own boss." That worked out for me pretty well. Since 2005, I've owned three six-figure businesses.

I've had moments of bravery, just surviving while living a life on the streets. I've had to be brave hearing the jail doors clang behind me. I've clung to bravery while surviving drugs, partying, booze, and some really low self-esteem. I finally made a massive leap, released the chains of pity, of fear of failure, and lack of self-love and turned my dreams into a reality. It is a result of the commitment I made to "doing the work" that I'm where I am today. My biggest moment was deciding unexpectedly to release the shame of my past of incarceration and homelessness during my first women's empowerment event. Shedding those chains and all that shame freed me and opened me up to the new life that was waiting for me. Releasing those chains, I now have room for abundance and light.

I draw from the strength of other courageous women. Despite everything, we don't know about other women warriors. Every day, it seems, more stories emerge of women who fought great fights on every social and economic level. More women are being acknowledged with awards and positions of power. We all need to know more about these women who showed us the way. Think about it, just the simple fact of knowing that life wouldn't be here without a woman is strength in itself. All things come from women; I feel lifted daily knowing that I have the ability to bring forth life.

My life's dream began as a little girl, when all I wanted to do was to work in TV and film. Back then I thought we are all filled with big dreams and massive gifts and that everybody wants to share those gifts with the world. As I grew older and my dreams got twisted, I understood that it's easy to get sidetracked. There is no greater pain in the world than wishing, wanting, and trying to make your dreams come true, yet being unable to do so. I thought my dream was not meant to be and that I didn't deserve it. I didn't feel worthy.

But somewhere along the line, my spirit reminded me that all change in life and in business comes from the inside out. When we dig deep and do the inner work it is then and only then that we attract more abundance than we ever could imagine. I believe there is nothing more fulfilling than seeing your dreams become a reality. Fast forward to now, and I am quite literally living my dream life after thirty years of being afraid of stepping into unfamiliar territory. I am now an actual filmmaker, sharing inspirational stories of women and men who have overcome trauma and come out triumphant on the other side.

I wouldn't do anything differently if I was given a chance. Maybe I'd try to look at the results of what I've done, decisions I've made, and think differently about those decisions while realizing that each loss is a lesson. My life is miraculous. It is filled with love. Like many, I've made plenty of bad decisions on my journey that could have cost me my life or freedom. Those decisions caused me to feel hopeless, sad, and empty with negative stories playing on a loop in my mind. I knew there was so much more out there, but I had no idea how to get there. The changes I have experienced, both in myself and my life, have blown me away.

The challenges I face now are getting people to spread positivity – personally, virally, and in every way, especially as a woman. I do believe if I was a man, others would respond at higher rates. But I won't let this stop me. I'm a big believer that all our desires in life can be achieved if we invest the time and energy into releasing our mental, emotional, and generational chains. Nothing in life will come to you if you are not ready to receive it.

The advice I am giving to my children is to think for themselves and to take what others tell them with a grain of salt. I want my kids to live, think, and speak loudly for themselves. I speak life into them daily so that they are inspired to live lives they love without being concerned or held back due to other people's ideas or judgments of them, even mine.

I cannot be stopped because I am here to guide and support people to clear out fear, activate their power, see all the possibilities for rock-solid lives, leave a legacy, and add more zeroes to their bank account! Call me unstoppable because I didn't let drugs, jail, homelessness, booze, or low self-esteem stop me in the past and *nothing* can stop me now!

UNSTOPPABLE
HEALING OF
Family and Community

"Unstoppable women know the power of a village. We don't leave anyone behind and we gain strength from one another. We raise ourselves to greater heights when we love—a mate, a child, a grandmother, a parent. We rise to greater heights when we commit to that love. These women steeped themselves in that love. It's a necessary part to happiness, and all these women, even after much struggle, found their happiness in just loving. That love gave them the fuel to struggle forward and keep struggling to get to where they want to be. Unstoppable love: it's the secret power."

~Bershan Shaw

Angela Collins Green

A single mother of eight children who raised them, and then herself.

I am a single mother to eight children. Having my first child at the age of nineteen wasn't scary at all. Just about everyone in my family had a teenage pregnancy and I was no different. I wasn't prepared at all but took on the challenge with this naïve idea of "I'll be fine" because I didn't know better. My life as a mother has been hell! Don't misunderstand me, I love my children but the cards of life that I was dealt were not a good hand to gamble, with children. I've had to become a grown woman right in front of my children, as well as a responsible mother my kids could be blessed to have. I never thought about that part when I read that positive pregnancy test. I had this idea that I was "grown." I have watched with gut-wrenching terror as my little girls suffered from my most non-mother and non-woman-like times. I have fought hard not to appear weak and inadequate in front of them, but I wasn't always so successful. I've fallen short on many important occasions in their lives, losing the "hero" cape they had naïvely given me. Their hero was not a hero. I was a failure.

At those moments I had failed myself and, more important, my children. I couldn't afford to pay for it all. I mean, what kind of trick was God playing on me? Yes, I made a mistake and had child after child while I was young, but God, I'm out here trying. Why have their fathers abandoned me? Why have they abandoned their children? Why is my fight so hard to fight, knowing I will remain alone? At times my conscience would call me selfish because I did not want to give my kids up even though I was having a difficult time raising them. I could suffer and be a lowlife, but my kids deserved a life in which running water, food, electricity, and clothes were never an issue. But I love my children and could never give them up. I know this because I tried. Twice.

I tried twice at two separate times in my life to rid my babies of a hard life. The first time was when I was younger. I had a few children by that time and was just hanging on to life. I was severely depressed but didn't know it. I was still in the hospital when I was blessed with a beautiful and healthy baby whom everyone complimented and deemed to be my most beautiful one yet. But I was screaming inside. I was looking into the eyes of a new life to whom I couldn't make any solid promises. Hell, I didn't even know how I was going to make it home with him after being discharged. When he was just two or three days old, and my milk pouring into my breast to nourish him, I decided that this child deserved better than me. I would do what was best for him and eliminate feelings from the equation.

On the last day of my stay at the hospital, one of the nurses wanted to help me discharge so she came to clean and dress my baby for our trip "home." I had no home. I was homeless. After she left with my beautiful boy, I proceeded to get dressed, with my mind made up to leave the hospital and leave my child. It wasn't strange to anyone that I hadn't seen my newborn for most of the day, but it was for me because I'm very protective over my children. I'm the mother that keeps the baby with me at all times. This time, however, I wasn't feeling at all like a mother. I wasn't feeling anything.

I wasn't going to put another child through my ill-planned highs and lows if it at all could be prevented. I had made up in my mind that I would accept the judgment and critical voices of those who ever found out what I had done. I was OK with the idea of "giving up'" my child so that he could have better than what I could provide. But fate didn't allow it. I needed a ride and, inexplicably, my mom had come. I had called a taxi but the snow that day was relentless! No taxis. I waited and waited with my fists clenching tightly to a plastic grocery bag filled with my belongings, a constant reminder as to why this decision was for the best. Still, no taxi came. I called two or three more cab companies to increase the likelihood of a ride "home," but nothing. I was getting nervous because at some point the nurse would return with my baby and notice that I had no plans to take this child with me. I thought, "Angela, just leave. Forget the papers and forget the cab. Walk away. What harm is a snowstorm?" I honestly wouldn't have felt the storm. I was emotionless and severely depressed. So I thought.

Depressed? Yes. Emotionless? Not even close. My feet planted firmly to the hospital room floor wouldn't budge. The image of my newborn baby's hands tightly balled up from the last time I had touched them kept replaying in my head. Those newborn hands were balled up just like mine were at that exact moment. This child was making me feel everything and all at once. I couldn't shake the feeling. It was as if my baby was fighting my decision and fighting for us. We both were fighting. Fighting for love to somehow inter-vene. Out of nowhere, my mom appeared and noticed a car seat full of stuff but no baby. All I could think was, "How is my mom here?" As I was about to leave, she walked in my room and said, "Where's the baby?" I was shocked into reality by the question but calmly replied, "Oh, the nurses are getting him ready for me." Then an aunt of mine also appeared and just waited in the room with me as some weird reinforcement to stay "planted." Maybe my child was praying for me? Had to be because I wasn't. God's reinforcement came. A prayer was answered. It was a divine moment indeed.

I had called no one and expected nobody to come for me that day. When my mother came into the room, she had a feeling that I had made a choice to leave without my child and said, "I'll go and get him, you stay here." She returned with my newborn, all cleaned up but still in a hospital undershirt. That image further confirmed her initial thoughts upon seeing me without a baby. God had other plans.

That moment changed the outcome of my infant child's life and mine forever. Destiny intervened, and I had to face all my fears head on. I chose love despite the fear I was facing. That day I'll never forget. My heart had been healed. Many, many counseling sessions provided a place to encourage that. My beautiful baby is a teenager now and we have never separated. His fight is just like mine. His desire to live is just like mine. What God allowed is a moment of great pain to teach me a great lesson. But that's a whole other story. . . .

Being a mother has been difficult but being a woman. Sad to say, I'm just learning what that role is all about. I have lived my whole life for my children and, as a result, neglected myself as a woman. The last five years of my life have been about discovering me, the woman—not the mother or the soon to be ex-wife. I have found throughout this journey that I am better at being a woman versus being a mother and a wife. Meaning: I love everything about me. I have found traits, gifts, and qualities in me that no one ever expressed or confirmed for me. Self-exploration at its finest is responsible for this. For me, becoming a woman has caused an uproar in my family. My immediate family is full of women who have sacrificed their lives for single motherhood, not in a good way. Many generations before us provided no examples of self-worth or value. Furthering your education and proper planning was never on the table. Toxic relationships and marriages were OK, as long as the money was right. That was my example growing up as a young woman. Very late, in my opinion, I finally decided to come out of that sick mindset. I took many self-help classes, went back to school, and found a few mentors along the way.

I discovered through this process that I was a woman who was not only beautiful but smarter than I had imagined. That revelation began to manifest in my life and made a lot of people uncomfortable. I came to a quick realization that I needed to be the woman to whom I had never been exposed. I found out that I was the only one who could save and guide me out of this grave that had been dug for me. Only I could get me out. Being a woman, standing in power and with a true identity, is a super-power.

Many years since have passed and my babies have grown up. I was able to get through many tough days and had met a man with whom I thought I would spend the rest of my life. I was so grateful to not just have a husband but a man to be a father figure to my young children. As I write this, my marriage is pending divorce. It's the best decision I have ever made. That relationship had created so many creative and love blockages in my own life as well as those of my children. I married my oppressor without being fully awake to this.

Going back to school was by far the most self-fulfilling experience. Although I can't ever seem to finish, I've embraced the journey. Through that I have found that I genuinely love to learn. I honestly wish I had valued school more as a young person and had the opportunity to stay in one school more than a few months at a time. Today, I take quick courses and study trainings to gratify my urges for knowledge. I read often and write in a journal a great deal. I have self-published a few books and plan to publish more. I host training retreats on self-love and life lessons. I need quick courses of study since it's all I can handle, being a single mother to eight vibrant children at the moment.

My life is just beginning. I have many dreams. One of those dreams is to help other women dig themselves out of what I like to call "slave graves" — graves that were dug by someone else for them or for some by their other half, the self-saboteur. I desire to help women like me get from stuck to unstuck. I believe in miracles because I am one. I will use every last one of my God-forbidden, self-loathing, inconceivable failures and excuses to save anyone and everyone who is willing to listen. I write. I speak. I encourage. I fail. I survive. I learn and live to die another day. That is my life's purpose.

I am happy in my current state. However, I am not satisfied. I won't be satisfied until I get what I came here for. I'm not sure of what that is, but I am in complete awareness that I have not attained it yet. It's a weird feeling to have—a feeling of reaching a premeditated destination yet realizing it's still not the place. That's my challenge today. The challenges I face from traveling a road of purpose without knowing its true destination can be quite overwhelming. But I am being propelled to just keep moving forward, and so that's what I do.

In conclusion, I hope to inspire my children and other women through my many defeats to pursue and live anyway. Live and push through the pain. The very first person I inspired and helped heal was me. I was a mess and I still have work to do, but that's what makes my real life a teeth-clencher. Will she make it? Truth be told, I already have.

Laquita Brooks

From realtor to motivational speaker on liberating boundaries.

I'll never forget the first time I stepped in front of a group of women who'd come to hear me inspire them with my words and experience. I was terrified—but I knew I was doing the right thing. Before that, I'd spent years as a realtor, selling millions of dollars' worth of property while managing three small businesses. I did all of that while making a welcoming home for my husband and three children. I was proud of my successes, but realized I wanted more: I wanted to help others be successful, too.

I made what was one of the scariest decisions in my life: I opted for change. I opted to change from what we women so often do: give up on our own wants and needs to take care of others. It's a mistake. We can have what we want and love in our lives. I put those guaranteed money-earning jobs aside and risked my family's stability to follow my dream of being a motivational speaker.

There is more to being a parent than just making babies and paying bills. This is what I learned with my own family. Babies don't ease your desire to be loved; as a matter of fact, it merely creates a vicious cycle where you transfer your frustration to your offspring. No one but you can love you better, and you must always fight rejection and break the chain of disconnection and find your self-love. No one taught me this. I had to learn myself and I guess that is why they say life is a teacher.

I became a mother at the age of 18, adding to the statistics of teenage mothers. The father of my daughter barely had time for us and, as a teenager who still had a long way to go, I did not know how to mother. I got married when she was at the age of six, and for a moment, I thought it would help, but it didn't. My husband was also a single father like me with a daughter one year younger than my girl, but unlike my girl, my step-daughter's mom was always there for her. She just didn't win in the bid to be the caregiver. My daughter felt more rejected and ignored. She felt she had been short-changed.

My daughter went way off the hook and became uncontrollable as she grew older. Her rebellion heighted each day and each year. I couldn't think of anything to do but send her to a therapeutic boarding school in Arizona. But when she came back, and we were all glad she was returning, she still was angry. I was heartbroken and felt like I had failed completely in my life.

After a few months, she moved in with her dad but naturally that was difficult too. All mothers fear three things for their teenage daughters: drugs and dealing, abuse, or teenage pregnancy. For my daughter, it was teenage pregnancy. She got pregnant at 19, a year older than I was when I had her. Now I became a grandma and had to care for her and my grandson and my entire family. Even so, she never let go of her anger at me, and I was still learning how to be a parent and grandparent.

My life taught me that babies are not baby dolls, they are not something you give back once you've had them. They are real and their responsibilities must be taken on wholeheartedly. Jumping into a relationship and opening yourself for sex doesn't make you feel loved. Now I know the best way to be loved is to find self-love. You must always fight for the life you really want, and you must fight bravely and wisely.

People who see me now are surprised to learn that I'm naturally shy and often uncomfortable speaking in front of large groups. They see me stand center-stage, microphone in hand, and they hear my clear voice, confidence infusing my words. They are unaware I am living proof that with support, with practice, with love, they, too, can follow their dreams. I still would like to travel more and maybe my business will be the vehicle for me to do that.

Today I help individuals and small groups find the pathways to their best lives, giving them permission to be great. I inspire. I push. I cheerlead. I guide. People call me "The Motivational Maven," and I'm proud of that nickname. Knowing I've helped people positively change their lives is what keeps me going when I have fears of my own. I'm not saying life is easy and that things always go right for me. I'm saying that I'm a fighter who believes waiting is a mistake and the time to live is now. I believe that living is about ongoing change and challenge. I think my mission is to help others break free of stagnation and soar. To think less fear, more courage.

Try something that scares you. Now, not later. Then do something else and something else. The journey might be rough, but understand the ups and downs are part of the process. Your woman-born resilience will see you through. When you reach one destination, scan the horizon for the next. And see yourself as beautiful and as great as those who love you see you.

Renee Marie Beavers
Honest, open, and transparent about the whys in life.

I am fifty-one years old and I am an unstoppable warrior woman. I like to remain honest, open, and transparent (HOT); it is how I thrive in relationships. If you asked, "How did you become the person you are today?" I would have to say I am a product of my choices and not my environment alone. Our choices form our habits and our habits shape our lifestyles. Many of us have had our share of disappointment, sadness, heartbreak, childhood of origin issues, rejection, betrayal, failure, and sickness. The $5-million question is, what will we do with it all? Do we unpack it all or do we act as if we're OK? The choice is ours to make but the effects affect everyone with whom we come in contact.

We all have the same basic needs. Love, belonging, security, and purpose are what connects us to one another and God. When we grow up in an environment in which any one of our core needs is left unmet, we find ourselves spending what could turn into a lifetime treating the symptoms without ever truly looking inward at the real unmet needs. Fear, anxiety, depression, anger, low self-esteem, pride, narcissism, and arrogance are only symptoms of deeper needs. No one can examine your heart except you. We waste valuable time chasing the symptom rather than facing ourselves and our issues head on. Blaming our unmet needs on external sources and other people is just as ineffective as pulling the leaves off a tree. It won't kill the tree itself, but it will leave it bare and exposed.

By choosing to play the blame game, we push people away and we miss out on what God wants to use to help us to grow and change—our relationships with others. Denial won't fill the emptiness inside our hearts. Acting as if nothing is wrong will not treat it either. When we don't try to figure out the origin of our embedded issues, we end up isolated and alone. Living alone is not a healthy long-term life strategy. There is more—and you deserve to experience it.

I was born to two drug-addicted parents in Detroit, Michigan, in 1967—the year of the Blood Race Rebellion Riots. among the most violent and destructive riots in U.S. history. My biological father left my mother and me before I was four years old, leaving me to live with my great-great-grandmother and my great-grandmother before I was bounced to my grandparents.

The next bounce was to my mother's oldest single sister and her three children. Talk about a turbulent start! I wish that was the end of my bumpy beginnings. Unfortunately, there is more. My biological father died when I was eleven. My godfather, whom I loved dearly, was murdered when I was a teenager. My stepdad, who loved me dearly and raised me as if I was his own blood, died of cancer when I was twenty-three. There is more.

My great-grandmother and my great-great-grandmother died before I was six years old. My godmother, whom I loved and treasured, died when I was twenty-two years old. My mom was murdered by a serial killer when I was twenty-three years old. My mother-in-law, who loved and who embraced me as if I were her own daughter, died when I was thirty years old.

Death appeared early and frequently in my life. Yet it has definitely been one of my greatest teachers. That is why I have learned to cherish life and love. Today, I choose to live my life for love. Sure, I spent years tracking and hashing through my past. At times, I found myself stuck in my unforgiveness and pain. Many days I felt sorry for myself, as if life was treating me unfairly. Each of these horrific events, if not unpacked, could have defined and destroyed me. I am strong and resilient not because the clock has moved on but because I have. I forgave. I ask for forgiveness. I love and I allow others to love me.

Life is unfair. We will all have horrible, tragic things that will happen in our lifetime and they will hurt us. What we do with our hurt is what differentiates and defines us. I like to give the bad news first, that's why I shared all my losses here first. I want to leave you with hope and something to look forward to. There is more. Here's the good news of my story: I met my husband Gil when I was fourteen; we worked a summer job together for the City of Detroit. We began dating exclusively at eighteen, got married at twenty-one, and had our amazing daughter at twenty-three. We also adopted my two little sisters after my mother was violently murdered when Gil and I were twenty-three.

My first Mother's Day, I had three children—interesting, right? Two young, poorly parented kids raising three kids. Looking back on it now, I am sure that God's love kept us. Our stability has always been portable. My husband was in the United States Air Force for twenty-three years. We lived in thirteen different cities. So, not only am I strong and resilient, I am also very flexible! I like to say, "She who is flexible is not easily broken." I have learned to look for the good even in bad situations. Change and starting over teaches you to be open to new people, places, and ideas. These are all good things.

My marriage to Gil is my happily ever after. I believe that God writes into all our stories good and bad, happy and sad. Gil is my best friend, my lover, protector, and my promise from God. He is a tangible reminder that God will never leave us or forsake us. I love my life and my story, they are my gifts to God. I am not unstoppable because I am fearless and brave; I am unstoppable because I will not quit! When I am knocked down, I get back up again. Yes, I bounce back. There is more. By 2011, I was diagnosed with three different autoimmune diseases. In 2015, after being fed up with all of the prescription drugs, pain, fear of dying, and feeling as if I were eighty years old, I decided to go on a water fast, which transformed my life.

I have struggled with food addiction and serial dieting since the age of eleven years old. You name a diet and I have been on it. Food, unlike my parents, was always available. I felt as if it was a comforting friend. What a lie! Food and things cannot love us back; they are designed to serve us. We must stop serving them! All the years of high-protein diets, taking supplements, and extreme "health" programs are what I believe are the biggest contributing factor to my vitiligo, celiac, and arthritis. I call these lifestyle diseases. After years of searching and trial-and-error, I believe that I have found my cure! Without discovering the cause, you will never find your cure. Prayer, fasting, and a whole-food, plant-based lifestyle have provided a clear solution to my unhealthy, ungodly relationship with food, myself, and others. There is more.

I am ninety percent pain free and I am not on any prescription drugs. I feel better and stronger than I ever have in my lifetime—physically, spiritually, and emotionally. Being an unstoppable warrior woman is about being vulnerable and HOT. I hope by sharing my story, you will be inspired to write, live, and own your story! From one unstoppable warrior woman to another, remember that no matter your stage in life, you do have control over your choices. Too many times we relinquish our power to people and things. The greatest human display of strength is self-control. Control your choices, your time, and your habits. These are the elements in life that connect and define us all. They are our most valuable commodities.

I challenge you to use your choices in ways that serve you well and empower you to develop the strength to serve God and others. That is the kind of success that brings hope, freedom, and liberty. We can't pick our families of origin, our DNA, or even our facial features. We can control our time, our choices, and our habits. Examine them, manage them, and, most important, own them! Remember, we are more alike than we are different. You are not alone! Your story, your pain, and your difficulty are not unique. However, you are and there is more.

Today, I am a Christ follower. I am a wife, mother, sister, friend, entrepreneur, author, and lifestyle strategist. With so many titles as women, it is crucial that we discover our "why." After owning and building salons for twenty-eight years, I had come to a personal realization: I found my identity not in my God-given purpose but in my ability to generate income. Living your life motivated by "how" and money is exhausting in our information-driven societies. There are millions of how-to's. Most of them will produce some results. Yet, "how" without "why" is like day without night; it is out of balance and it will wear you out.

Learning "how" to achieve a task or goal is also somewhat easy to do if we take the long journey inward to discover our "why." "Who" will rule our life and crowd our intimacy with God, ourselves, and others. I loved doing hair and I was good at it; and yes, I made a lot of money. If you asked me during that time about my life, I would have shared that I was living "my best life." The key word is that I was living my best life! Not for God, but for me and mine only. Being comfortable can be so dangerous. In our comfort, we are not dependent on hearing God or even asking Him for our next step. I would always brag and say that I could do hair with my eyes closed. That's a very dangerous place to remain. We grow when we are stretched, challenged, and uncomfortable.

God will call each of His children out into the deep, off the sidelines, and, yes, to do something that makes us feel uncomfortable. Today, I am becoming the woman that God designed me to become. All the things that scared me to death are now a part of my daily life. I write books and I speak on radio, on television, and in small groups and in one-on-one sessions. Why, how, who? Yes, the once very insecure, overweight girl with low self-esteem is now thriving in an environment where she was born to belong. (Although, I must admit that I would have never picked this life for myself.) After writing four books and sending out hundreds of press releases, holding radio interviews in my closet (to achieve great sound quality), and being told no thousands of times, I can say with certainty that this is what I was created for.

If I have learned only one lesson worth sharing it is that unpacking your "why" is liberating. Why do I get up each day not knowing the outcome but still have hope and joy each day? My "why" is that God loves me, and He loves everyone around me— even the people that I don't know or like. God wants to use my mess, my pain, and my failures. All I have to do is willingly give them to Him and He turns them into something beautiful. I hope that by living God's life in the power of my "why," my unpacked life will encourage you to discover your "why." What do I mean by unpacked? I will give you an example. For years, I lost and gained weight, had unresolved conflicts with people, and did not know how to use my voice for good. I had to ask myself, "Why?" What is the common thread in these seemingly different events? Me, it's me! I cannot control anyone or anything around me. My "why" is for me.

Why don't I use my power and energy to change me? Why don't I set boundaries, limits, and have realistic expectations for myself and others? Why don't I learn to say no to myself and others? Why have I wasted so much time? Why can't I forgive? Why can't I ask for forgiveness? I basically asked myself "why" until there were no questions left. I call this unpacking yourself. Our "why" is the key to finding peace and solutions.

Tameka Hope
A world ripped apart by a giant tornado.
Survivor in the storm.

*M*y saddest and most challenging moments all happened during one horrifying event, when a large and violent multiple-vortex tornado hit my hometown of Tuscaloosa, Alabama. It raced all the way between Tuscaloosa and Birmingham, hitting all the smaller communities and rural areas between the two. It is one of the costliest tornadoes on record and was one of the 360 tornadoes in the 2011 Super Outbreak, what Wikipedia states as the largest tornado outbreak in United States history. Imagine the terror we went through; this was the third tornado to strike the city of Tuscaloosa in the past decade, and the second in two weeks. The tornado destroyed my home and my whole neighborhood in less than ten minutes. Nothing was left but the foundation of my house.

It left me, our three kids, and their dad homeless. It took a different kind of bravery just to endure the aftermath of the storm.

We needed to somehow put our lives back together. We stayed wherever we could. Friends, family, and strangers blessed us with money, food, clothes, and furniture. It was a struggle to gather new identification papers, birth certificates, and all the personal things that were blown away by the tornado. You take so many things for granted until you reach for them and they are not there, even the simplest things like a toothbrush, a way to wash your face, a snack for your babies.

As my kids struggled to understand what had happened, we struggled to explain that life throws tests and trials at you. We were trying to give them courage and hope for a better day. Yet we felt like we were failures as parents. We didn't have any insurance money and no money in the bank to get a new home for our kids. It felt impossible to find a permanent home as we went from motel to motel. This tornado not only ripped apart our home, it seemed to have blown away all my emotional stability. I was running from the personal pain of losing everything. And became very disturbed and overtaken by anxiety and depression and started dealing with it by self-medicating. Some days I would be so high off medications and over-the-counter cold and cough medicine that it would seem like parts of my body were numb. Panic attacks would come out of nowhere, kicking in when I was by myself. I kept seeing people's body parts mixed in with debris from the storm.

I think the challenge of holding a family together in times of stress and despair is a challenge for many people. For us, it had all become so overwhelming that my husband and I would argue constantly, saying hurtful things to one, another blaming each other for our struggle. We were on the brink of divorce and had to decide whether we'd give up or make it together. We had to find a way to get through those issues and keep the marriage together. Often when we were about to get back on track, it turned into that old saying: one step forward, two steps back.

Our self-worth was at an all-time low. At the point we were so overwhelmed from asking people for help that we just decided not to anymore. We began to pray as a family and ask God for strength to make it through and to endure all we had to face. Slowly, things would get a little better, and then they'd get even worse. But we kept reminding ourselves that if we could survive the force of a hurricane, we could get through whatever was thrown at us.

But it makes you crazy when you can't even get basic needs for your children. Having your utilities disconnected is something nobody should have to endure; when they came to turn off our water, I just sat there in tears. Times were so hard; my husband was fired from his job. Our car was repossessed when we were out shopping with our kids. We came out of the store and the car was gone. We hadn't even had the car a month but we didn't have insurance for it, so they took it back without telling us what was happening.

My husband was so upset he threw the car keys across the parking lot. I was just standing there thinking, trying to keep my tears from falling in front of our kids. But we got through all this, holding on to each other. My marriage is strong. If the tornado couldn't blow it apart, nothing can. That's a message the world needs to hear also.

I think it's harder for a woman to be taken seriously when she is filled with big dreams. I was always laughed at and talked about with silly, often cruel jokes because nobody believed me when I told them I was going to start my own business, write books, songs, design clothes, and create inventions. As I moved through tough times, it was harder to look to a future nobody thought a woman could have.

Being the matriarch of my household, balancing my relationship with God and somehow still believing in myself and my dreams and goals has lifted me up as a woman. Being a woman has allowed me to give birth to three wonderful children. As a woman, I love to walk fearlessly in my dreams and goals at this point of my life.

I am happy to be alive and to be at a place in my life where I am willing and ready to walk in my God-given purpose! I am not where I desire to be right now due to my finances and the right guidance to get things going and out to the world. But I want to share my testimony with the world and help all the people who suffer in silence day to day because they too have lost everything to some type of natural disaster like tornados, floods, or hurricanes.

I have not succeeded in my dreams because there is still so much work that I must do. I would like to introduce so many of my visions and products to the world. My main dream is to travel the world to share my testimony of overcoming depression and suicidal thoughts caused by the severe weather and the resulting tragedy. I would like to share how it has changed my life and my family's life to understanding other people's needs and cries for help. I want all the people around the world who have experienced something similar to start celebrating the anniversary of those events as a time to celebrate life.

I want to tell the world that life's tests and trials come to build you up and push you into your true destiny and purpose! I succeeded in writing and publishing a book called God Had Other Plans. It has been described as an "emotional and empowering memoir [that] proves that you can chase your dreams, achieve your goals, and be all that your heart desires in spite of life's unexpected circumstances."

I've also become an entrepreneur with a company called Faithful Printing & Apparel, which I'm very proud of—but I have not accomplished my goals to be walking in my full purpose. I have many dreams that remain unfulfilled: launching a hair product invention; lip gloss, jewelry, and shoe lines; ladies, men's, and children's clothing lines; and even a luggage line. You know, all those things that people laughed at when I was young. I also have dreams to make my book God Had Other Plans into a movie or play to help others around the world.

If I could go back in time, I would have left my hometown and followed my dreams. I would have not had an abortion as a teenager; I would have been strong enough to speak my truth about wanting to keep my baby. Having that abortion really weighed on me for years and I never told my parents. I used to think about how old the baby would be as I counted the years that passed. I became kind of emotional as I saw other classmates with their kids. There was a time when I used to cry when I was alone, but with the passing of time, I'm more at peace with myself.

The struggles I face today are due to my past health issues and operations. Living with poor health is my challenge. It's hard to stand for a long period of time and I have ongoing issues in my back and legs due to fibromyalgia. I nearly died from a serious infection after surgery in 2011. That was followed by four emergency surgeries.

We still face the challenge of getting our family fully back on our feet so we can set out to do all we dream of, but God's favor and grace has kept and covered us. We have found a place in my hometown to stay until we are blessed to be able to buy our own home with enough room that's fully furnished.

As a mother, I have over the years tried to be home more for my children because they need me and need my advice that would serve where they were in life at that time. Now that they are in the beginning stages of teen years and are beginning to figure out who they are, I tell them to always keep God first and treat others how they want to be treated and to believe in who and all God has created them to be. I tell them not follow what others are doing but to be different, create their own lane.

Clearly, not even a tornado the size of Alabama can stop me. I am unstoppable.

Pamela G. Sharpe
Life gives you what you believe you deserve.

I've been private all my life. I have never wanted anyone to really know my truths, my failures, sins, bad decisions, and hurts. These were my mistakes, sins, and shame. Not something to display for everyone to examine and talk about. The first time Bershan Shaw asked me to write about something I had never told anyone, I began to panic. I sat there looking at the screen, feeling afraid, numb, anxious. I knew this was a defining moment.

As I began to write, I became overwhelmed, and tears started slowly falling, then more and more. I had to stop several times, but I continued. I wrote and released some of the shame I had been carrying. As I wrote, I began forgiving the people in my story and then I forgave myself. I asked God to forgive me and release the pain so that I could share my story and help others to grow. As I wrote, I thanked God for helping me to overcome myself, for giving me strength to move from that situation. As I wrote,

129

I began to feel a sense of peace flow over me. I was not embarrassed anymore. My past is part of my journey, lessons I had to learn, courage and faith that had to grow inside of me. I felt a release from the past.

Now, I can write about the past, and I also reference my journey in speeches, social media posts, in my upcoming book, and during conversations. These are my part of my Divine Purpose. Examples that I use to help people move past all the yesterdays and into today. I've learned that I am not the only one who has had these type (and even worse) of experiences. I've learned that sharing my story opens others to share and release the hurt, pain, and guilt that they are carrying. I've learned that once it's out, then the real work begins. That's when real courage shows up.

I have always loved being a woman but I've held myself back by believing in lies and allowing those lies to invade my life. It hasn't been the fact that I am a woman that was holding me back. It was believing I was unworthy, less than, not smart enough, not pretty enough, and so on. The bigger problem has been worrying about what others would think or say about me. Would they like me? Would they accept me? I had been living in fear of being unacceptable, found out, not good enough. I allowed these untruths to take root in my mind. These lies led to fear, which led to procrastination, which led to playing small. Every day, I must remind myself that I am worthy. I can do it. I am strong. I am beautiful. I am smart. Just do it. Move. I can do anything that I put my mind to doing. That I have within me everything that I need to succeed in life.

I learned that there is power in the female soul and spirit. Our internal guidance system, *intuition*, is strong. We are inherently spiritual and in that spirit is love. I am a mother to three children and motherhood has been my greatest joy. Infinite and eternal love is always there. This love has kept me grounded and strong. This love has given me courage and confidence. The ways in which women love each other is uplifting. No, it is beautiful. The way women go out of our way, to love, honor, support, cry, lift, encourage, and feel for each other is indescribable.

Women can discern when another woman is hurting and are able to offer the right words, hugs, or gift that will lift her up. My mother, daughters, aunts, grandmothers, mother-in-law, sister-in-law's, and sister-friends have and are always here to offer encouragement, build my confidence, hold me accountable, provide clarity, trust, friendship, and love. Being a woman is being in an exclusive love club. Women are the foundation for new beginnings, growth, rebirth, and forgiveness. Woman have a strength and love that cannot be measured. It is infinite. Just when you think you can't, you pull from the inner strength and spirit and find that you can. I am a woman and I know I can soar, because I am spiritually complete.

I am a work in progress. Living every day is a dream, a grand adventure. I am so happy with the direction I am headed in. The dream keeps growing because my dreams are not as grand as God's plan for me. I believe God's dream for me is so much bigger and better than I could ever imagine. My dream is to live my life consciously, spiritually, and to be guided in everything I do by love and gratitude.

My dream, which is my Divine Purpose in life, as shown to me during meditation, is to be an in-demand spiritually uplifting speaker, coach, and entrepreneur. My dream is to travel the world, spreading the truth, that within you is a power that will allow you to manifest and create the life of your dreams. That everyone of us is more powerful than we know. That no one must live a life of limitation, lack, disease, or sadness. To teach people that life is a grand adventure and each and every day is a gift. The mindset with which you open the gift is how your day will be. To spread the word that your service to others is where your true success will be found. What you give, you get back tenfold. To teach people to just try. To want more and be more. To teach people that thoughts are energy. This energy goes out and manifests whatever you continuously think about. Thoughts truly become things. To teach people that we all are spiritual beings, connected, and our first nature is love. To teach people to love themselves and, in doing so, you will love others and others will love you. I'm so excited to see where this adventure takes me. "I am open and receptive to all the awesomeness the Universe has to offer, and I accept it, *now!*"

I have joy and peace of mind in knowing that I am loved by the Infinite Creator of all. I have a wonderful family that loves me and whom I love with all my heart. I am so grateful for my life, and everyone and everything in it. I am grateful and happy for each day that I wake up. I have wonderful friends who love me, and whom I love dearly. My life is good, and my biggest challenge is staying spiritually mindful each day, all day. Focusing on being in action towards my Divine Purpose and not getting in my head and allowing fear to keep me from my purpose. Moving past all fear and moving forward courageously and confidently towards my dream. I am 100 percent committed to trusting my inner spirit. When I do, my life is a wonderful adventure of manifestation, service, giving, and abundance. Then, I trust my intuition and follow the signs. I stay focused on the things I know are true, live fully and faithfully in my divine purpose, love myself fully, put being loving, kind, confident, intentional, adventurous, and courageous first. I play *big*! Unapologetically!

I tell everyone to put love first. Wake up with an attitude of gratitude, be grateful for everyone and everything. That every day is a present, open it with gratitude and a smile. Find time to get in touch with the spirit by meditating and praying at least twice a day. Happiness is found within, not on the outside. Motivation dies, but inspiration is eternal. Be inspired, in-spirit. Love and honor yourself. Trust your inner voice, it is God speaking to you. You are more powerful, strong, courageous, forgiving, and confident than you know. Thoughts become the things in your life. What you put in is what you will get back. Do not hate anything or anyone. Always forgive. Always. Be kind to yourself, say nice things about you and others. Be a good friend. Do not judge others. Be intentional, know what you want, and focus only on what you want. Choose to be positive and kind! Everything you need you already have within you. Fear isn't real, it is only a thought, move past it! Once you do the thing you are afraid of, you find that it was nothing. Step out on faith, believe in yourself, and *be you*! Be you! Be you! Breathe. Say thank you, always, and mean it. Apologize first. It's not always about you. Take responsibility for your beliefs, actions, choices, and words. Say no to things you do not want to do or have in your life. Do your best. Instead of being right, be kind and loving.

Always forgive yourself and others. Let go of the past, of people who are not right for you, and things and opportunities that are not in alignment with who you are and what you want in life. Let go of bad attitudes and negative responses. Stop making bad choices, and instead listen to your intuition. Pray and choose wisely. Allow others to be who they are on their own journey. Focus on the things you want and let go of everything else! Check your ego. Live intentionally, know what your goals are, update them regularly, and focus on them. Visualize your greatest life every day. Act as if you are the person and living the life you want to live. Keep your mind focused on God and the things that you want. Do not be selfish, give. God's storehouse is infinite. Let go of people who are not your champions. Stop trying to fit a square into a circle. Let it or them go! Flip the script on negative self-talk, negative people, and negative situations. There are no failures, only results. This is your journey. Learn the lessons. Instead of asking, "Why me?" ask "What is the lesson for me?" Treat people better than you want to be treated. Respect is found within, not without. Find a reason to smile every day!

LaShawn Butler

**Survivor of systemic and institutional oppression.
Toughened by four years of ugly custody battles.**

*T*he heart of what I do—supporting and empowering those who are often voiceless and invisible—propels me in my work as therapist, mentor, educator, and supervisor. Being brave every day became a necessity for survival. Maybe it came when I decided to write a book. I wanted to show people who have encountered all types of battles in their lives that they can survive and thrive. I wrote the book Holding On (2017) because there were so many days when that was literally all I could think to do. I found out so much about myself. I was constantly reminded of how much God was working when I couldn't muster up the energy to keep going. From the process getting accepted into New York University's Silver School of Social Work to graduating with honors while my life was constantly evolving, all of it was part of His bigger plan.

I am not certain that I was held back because I was a woman.

I think being a woman of color has held me back when pursuing my career. Before coming into social work I was studying to be a speech and language pathologist. I don't remember the exact words my professor used, but after going to her to say that I was struggling in her course, I decided (or she decided for me) that I would be more useful in the field of social work. I was twenty-two and still learning who I was at the time. Looking back, I would have handled her feedback differently.

Being a woman has lifted me up in so many ways. I was twenty-four years old when I lost my mother (who was thirty-nine—my age now) to inflammatory breast cancer. Our last year together was one of our best. My mother knew she wasn't going to beat cancer, so she was sure to give me and my siblings the tools we needed to live without her. It was that last year that my mother apologized for the mistakes she made and asked me to become a better version of her. It was life changing and I live for it daily.

My dream was to write. I wrote and published my first book. And while I dreamed of being an author, I had no idea that my book would be about my four-year long custody battle. But I knew that it would inspire others. Over 1,300 copies sold independently so far. I have had the opportunity to speak in front of many different audiences, from teen mothers to leaders in South Africa. My life has changed because I've seen my dream come true.

If I could go back to 2010, after being accepted to NYU, I would not have allowed my son to stay with his father while I earned my master's degree. Yes, my dream of becoming an author came true, but it was four horrific years that I am still processing today. Yet every day I wake up excited about another opportunity to work toward another goal. Even on the days that I am tired I thank God that I am able.

Currently, I am in the process of getting my private practice off the ground, planning my wedding, and preparing for age forty. Yes, these are all good things. The challenge is balancing it all. My son is in his junior year of high school, so I've been involved in getting him ready for his senior year. I have a full-time job and eleven clients that I see outside of that. Life is busy—good busy, but busy.

I would like to figure out a way to forgive my son's father. I am pretty sure we will never be friends or perhaps not even cordial because I haven't yet been able to forgive him for all that he did to me. Some days I think it's holding me back. I also know that my son would benefit from it, but I haven't built up the courage to accept his apology and move on. Fifty-six court appearances, a false arrest, and the lies that came along with it all—it is a little hard to get past all of this, but I'm hopeful.

Every day I tell my twenty-three-year-old and sixteen-year-old to make good decisions. I tell them not to be careless and don't think for one second that the decisions they make today will not affect their lives later. I was a teen mom and had both of my children by the time I was twenty-two. I had to grow up with them and that causes a whole lot of growing pains for everybody. I want my children to live, travel, and climb to the top of their careers before starting a family. While I don't regret the decisions that I made, I wish there had not been so many difficult times that came with those decisions.

People often look on the outside and see everything you want them to see. As a society, it happens far more often than we would like to admit. Holding On is a sobering reminder that life gets messy and it doesn't always look pretty. But with the right resources, mindset, and knowledge, you can make the inside and outside match. I have built a career in social work helping others, identifying resources and support services. That means nothing if I don't share it with those who need it. And we can never stop.

Shurvone Princess Wright
Leap of faith: The nurse who jumped into finance.

I am loving being over fifty. I feel like I have gotten into my groove in life, and I love that I am not afraid to be me! My smartest moment was when I left an abusive man when I was in my early twenties. I married him when I was twenty-one years old, and the moment I said, "I do," I felt a deep knowing in my gut that it was a mistake. I soon found out why: He became verbally abusive and, soon after, physically abusive. I had just finished nursing school when we got married, so I was feeling pretty confident in my accomplishments. However, after being with him for two years, I was scared and I developed low self-esteem. He would verbally abuse me in public and at home. One day, I said something he didn't like. He walked into the restroom where I was and knocked me on the floor. I passed out for a few seconds; when I came to, I remembered, "Wow, I am in trouble." I also remember thinking I wanted to kill him, or he would kill me.

Over the next few months, I developed a plan to leave. I started by gathering all my important papers together, hiding them in the closet. One day when he was at work, my auntie and her friend picked me up in a car large enough to hold my clothes and a few other belongings. I left him that day and never looked back. I was terrified, and I cried for six hours straight that night because I just did not know what I was going to do.

Deciding to live instead of waiting to die gave me the courage I needed to leave him. I had to start over with only the clothes I had and one paycheck. I moved back into my grandmother's home and started from scratch. I didn't have a car or anything other than what we had packed in the car. Once I found a job, I used public transportation to get to work. I ended up getting a good job, a car, and eventually my own apartment. It took a lot for me to leave and start over with nothing. I had to rebuild my life, my self-esteem, and my joy.

Sometimes I feel like being a woman—a petite Black woman, at that—has held me back because of society's perceptions. There have been times when people did not take me seriously because of my small stature, so I've always felt like I had to do better, act better, and perform better than my peers. As a Black woman, I did not always receive the same treatment as women of other ethnic origins in the workplace and in general. There were opportunities that were not offered to me. I have always known that I would have to work hard. In light of these feelings, I have worked tirelessly to get ahead. I don't let it hold me back; I have always looked for opportunities and taken advantage of anything offered to me in order to help advance my life.

Being a woman has lifted me up and has allowed me to lift others up with me. Women, in general, are amazing, strong, beautiful, and powerful human beings. We have a strength that is unmatched. I love connecting, hanging out, fellowshipping, and encouraging women. I have been involved in women's ministry off and on for about eighteen years. I've organized several women's conferences at my church, and I started my own women's ministry to encourage women to walk in their power. Being a woman has allowed me to connect with other women: that helps my soul. Women understand things men cannot; girlfriends are a source of comradery that we need as women in today's world.

I love being a part of the Unstoppable Warrior Woman Movement because I know that as a group, we can move mountains; we can encourage each other and support each other through difficult times. The energy and support motivate me to keep going after my dreams. Being a part of this movement, and the others I support, has made me more confident in my capacity for success: I love knowing that I have other women in my life who care about me and love to see me succeed. I love giving back to women, as well. I started a support group called Confidence Without Regret, which not only helps women walk in their purpose, but also uplifts me as I uplift others.

I have multiple dreams and I have succeeded in a few of them. One is seeing my daughters through college: Two daughters are graduates, and one is still a student. My second dream is to write a book, and I am making that dream come true. The Unstoppable Warrior Women Project is the third project to which I am contributing.

Another dream is to stop being afraid to dream. I left my nursing career to pursue a profession in the world of finance. It was scary, but my dream was to be successful and to stop letting fear get in my way. I am walking my dreams out in my life now, and

I am continuing to work on many more. Everything I have done in my life—the good, the bad, and the ugly—has shaped me and given me the courage to do what I am doing now in my life. Of course, I would want to skip feeling the pain I've felt in my life, but I would not change it.

I am happy and grateful for all that I have, all that I have worked for and all that God has given me. I am healthy, my kids are healthy, my husband and I have been married for twenty-five years, I have a home, a car, food, clothes, and a warm bed. How could I not be happy? I have come to learn that I can choose to be happy in any situation, good or bad. It has taken me a long time to get to this place, a knowing that I have a choice to be happy. Once you realize that you have a choice, life is different, and when you are faced with challenges you can decide to find that happy place.

After more than thirty years in nursing, I took a leap of faith and left to partner with an insurance company in order to start my own financial practice. I am still getting used to being a business owner instead of an employee. I am facing challenges regarding life's transitions: my husband recently turned sixty years old, and he is having a hard time, which, in turn, can be challenging for me at times.

One of my daughters is headed to an out-of-state college for four years for her graduate degrees, and for the first time in twenty-five years, my income dropped as I transitioned to walking in power and running my own business. There are so many moving parts, and sometimes it is overwhelming. I do a lot of praying, meditating, positive self-talk, and connecting with amazing women. I also face challenges in my business. The financial industry is made up mostly of men, so I must work extra hard to get ahead. I don't mind because I am used to going above and beyond. I also face the challenges of reaching the next level in realizing my vision, reaching more people, and making connections with the right people to help me continue to grow my business and reach my potential.

At this point, I would not change anything about my life. A few years ago, I might have said I would change many things, but as I've gotten older, I've come to realize that my life was destined to be what it is now. I believe that everything happens for a reason; if I changed things from the past, I wouldn't be where I am today. There have been times in my life when I did not think I would get through a particular journey, but prayer and a "never give up" attitude have always helped me to figure out a way to get things done. I believe that I am stronger and wiser because of the challenges I have faced. Even when I faced horrible situations, each of those experiences—good and bad—molded me into the person I am today.

The advice I give my daughters now is to continue to believe in what they want to do in life, stay positive, and remember that everything always works out. I tell them to create their lives and visualize their successes. I also tell them that if they don't communicate with me, then I cannot help: if they are honest with me, we can figure things out together. I encourage them to go out and be who they want to be, no matter what it is. I want them to love themselves and speak their minds. I have always challenged my girls to pursue their dreams, no matter what those dreams are, to work hard, and to never give up, ever! When faced with a challenge, take a step back, write things down, process the information, and then move forward.

One of the biggest things I had to overcome in my life was growing up around adults who used drugs. Learning how to survive in that environment was not easy. My grandmother raised me from the time I was born until I was eighteen years old; however, my mother and father would pick me up on and off throughout my life, whenever one of them had their life together long enough and well enough to take care of me for a time. During my stays with my mother, I witnessed her and the people she was around using drugs. I saw her being abused and taken advantage of in so many ways. It was heartbreaking because I felt helpless and afraid all the time. I always felt like I had to be perfect in order to avoid upsetting the man she was with so that he wouldn't abuse her. At the same time, I felt like I had to take care of my mom so that she would hopefully make better decisions and not antagonize the men in her life. Thinking about it now, it was a very dysfunctional situation. During these years, I became very shy and afraid of many things. It took hard work to overcome that obstacle and not become a product of my situation.

I have several role models. One is my husband Roger, because he provides unconditional love. He cheers me on in every single one of my endeavors. He has always shown me love and support, even at times when I did not deserve it. He not only loves me unconditionally: he shows his daughters the same love and support. No matter what, he is always there for them. He has a giving heart and is always helping others.

My other role models are my mom and grandmother, even though the relationship that I had with my mom was dysfunctional growing up. I am amazed at her strength, and the courage it took for her to become the woman she is today. She survived all that she has gone through and she has created a happy life for herself. She is a wonderful grandmother and mom. She is the kindest person I know. She managed to escape the abuse and a drug-infested life. I know she faced many hard days, but she never gave up. I believe

I get my strength and "never give up" attitude from her. Through all that she has gone through in life – abuse, drugs, and many other horrific things – she never gave up on life and never gave up on doing her best to love us.

My grandmother is another strong woman that I look up to. I had the honor of being raised by her. She raised six children before I came into this world, and she still took me in. She was a nurse for twenty-five years; during that time, she raised children, got married, purchased two homes, and kept them both until she passed at the age of ninety-three. She was a very strong and courageous woman who loved God and never gave up on life, no matter what. She showed me unconditional love and support, always. What I loved about her was that in the face of so many challenges, she always stayed calm, and somehow, things always turned out OK. She was the woman who introduced me to prayer and church. I believe in God because of my grandmother. I know how to pray because of my grandmother. I became a nurse because of my grandmother. I get my strength from her.

What I see for my future is another book. I want to write a story about the adoption of my two daughters. My daughter Destiny Faith was adopted at four years old, and my daughter Rebekah was adopted soon after she came home from the hospital as a newborn. I gave birth to Danielle. I want to write about the journey we've been on as a family and share the girls' perspective on the journey, too. I would also like to include Destiny's biological mom and grandmother. I want to have a book that offers multiple perspectives on how adoption affected their lives. I can see myself appearing on talk shows, doing speaking engagements, and being very successful in my financial planning business. I see myself coaching women around the world on how to live a courageous life without fear. I see myself going on book tours, and living a full life that helps others to soar as they execute the visions they have for themselves and their families. I want to continue to be a source of support for other women.

What makes me an unstoppable warrior woman is having the strength and courage to never give up on my dreams and vison. No matter what happens in my life, I will find the strength to get through it. I will always go after my goals with a passion and a purpose. Being an unstoppable warrior woman means you support women on all levels, lifting them up and encouraging them to be the best they can be. Being an unstoppable warrior woman means mentoring others and being a woman who helps others level up!

Michelle Greer
The beating heart of family.

*S*ometimes you need luck and that what's I used when I decided to return to school to pursue my undergraduate degree less than two months after the death of my husband. Just two days after his death, my acceptance papers arrived. Although I was fearful and certainly grief-stricken, I registered for summer classes as a full-time student. For the next eleven years, I juggled being a full-time student, full-time community advocate, full-time employee, and full-time single mom.

Becoming and being a widow is a nightmare that can't be explained. You never truly wake up from it; instead, you transmute with it, through it, and because of it. But you are never the same person. In fact, it feels like you never quite return to a sense of personal knowing. Rather, you are ejected into a very lonely journey of self-discovery that never ends. Now this may seem like normal everyday living on the surface, but it truly isn't. Self-discovery for a widow—particularly a young widow with two small children – feels more like a perpetual undoing and redoing. Just when you think you see a person vaguely familiar in the mirror, at the very next glance, you see someone you don't recognize at all.

Taking the step of returning to college as an adult single mom with young children was tough enough, let alone being the mother of a disabled child and being widowed following a beautiful relationship of nearly twenty years. I started dating my husband when I was sixteen; I had spent more years of my life with him in it than without him at the time of his death.

When I lost John, my heart was ripped from my chest. My entire world was crushed. It is, to this day, the most horrific experience of my life. And it continues to be the single-most impactful experience of my life. I lost my faith when I lost John, but I found a willpower in myself that I continue to rely upon. When I reflect, I can't really remember making it through; I just remember the feeling of having to make it through.

The experiences of womanhood have often made my life more challenging. The very nature of being a woman means that I possess emotions and often explore considerations in my decision-making that society has unfortunately stigmatized. We are the nurturers, the caregivers, and the wind beneath the wings of all we hold dear. Because we feel and move in a more caring and careful way, womanhood becomes our stumbling block. These experiences aren't unique, but these obstacles to our success are commonplace. In circumstances surrounding the loss of my husband, I was often treated like I was using grief to get a handout as opposed to simply receiving warranted consideration. Sometimes as women, we are forced to fight harder, to act harder, and ultimately, to become harder.

I believe society has finally begun to recognize that the stigma attached to womanhood no longer holds us back; rather, it holds society back. Women have always been the beating heart of family, community, and humanity. We have finally committed ourselves to bringing our gifts and contributions to the open eyes of all who care to see, and even to those who choose to close their eyes. Make no mistake about it: we have always been present, and we have always been strong. I am simply one story among many, bearing witness to the unstoppable greatness of womanhood.

I am certain that the stumbling blocks associated with my being a woman have always existed and will probably always exist, but I don't have time to ponder them. I only have time to keep reaching, keep fighting, and keep moving forward and upward.

Being a woman is uplifting, nevertheless. I am a fighter with compassion; I am a motivator because I have experienced the power of being motivated; I am an inspiration because I fully embrace and feel inspiration. Womanhood is a powerful yin to the yang. We are the proverbial two sides of the same coin. At our very best, we are that balance that the world needs, and we aren't at our best being anything other than who we are naturally. I am uplifted by the many beautiful experiences of being a woman: motherhood and sisterhood foster an incredible invisible thread that seems to transcend our differences. It's that something that we all grow to recognize, appreciate, and celebrate as woman power.

I have succeeded in my life's dream of becoming an attorney, but the dream of being the best attorney I can be is a continual endeavor. I have successfully acquired the tools needed to fulfill my God-given purpose. Now, my life's work has begun, and the fulfillment of that dream is something that I pray will outlive me.

Given the chance, I would definitely live more, because now I see that there have been many times when I wasn't—at least, not to the fullest, and not in all the ways that truly count. I have learned that against the backdrop of life, true meaning can be found in our ability to give and receive love amidst the highs and lows. Losing my husband allowed me to walk on the other side of death. When life is truly at its end, we don't regret not having things; we regret uncherished and unclaimed opportunities to give and receive love. Truly living is loving, and if given the chance to do it all over again, I would live to love fully and unconditionally—thereby loving life.

I am blessed. For me, happiness is a state achieved from within. I feel it as a frequent experience as opposed to a constant. However, I am always experiencing gratitude. I love me, I like me, and I experience happiness every day in being true to myself and my purpose in life. I feel happiness because I know unspeakable sadness up-close and personally.

Every day, I feel the emptiness of John being gone. I feel the emptiness in my children and my grandson not being able to spend time with him. I feel his absence during hallmark events in our lives. The anniversary of his passing still touches and clings to me as deeply as our wedding anniversary. And yet, the sadness of losing him seems to make the happiest moments with him shine brighter; that makes me miss him even more. I fear losing my loved ones, especially my mother and children. I fear them losing me. These are the scars left behind by sudden death and widow-hood. Living to love and loving life are lessons in which I have earned an A+, but it's the stuff of life that happens in between that challenges me.

Who wouldn't change everything in their life to reflect what they know now, or at least what they believe would be make life perfect? Unfortunately, life is indeed a mystery, and we seldom knew in the past what we know with some certainty in the present. If pressured to give an answer, I would say like most, I would get rid of all my bad experiences and replace them with good ones. But I'm not a little girl anymore; I know that those types of fairytales don't come true. Instead, my answer is that I would apply all that I have learned to make better decisions than were within my power yesterday. My way of doing the impossible is to apply that wisdom moving forward. Every day, I change my yesterday by making the best decisions within my power and accepting those things that I simply have no power or right to change.

After their dad passed away, I told my children when they were seven and eleven to love heavily and live lightly. I have taught them to listen to their hearts, to take heed of that little voice inside, and to treat others the way they want to be treated. I have taught them that if there is a cure to all life's woes, love is that elixir. I have demonstrated and in turn expected them to always find meaning and some way to bring good out of tragedy. When John passed, my children and I became ambassadors for stroke awareness and prevention. We told John's story and our own with the intention of seeing our tragedy become someone else's blessing. Today, almost every hospital in Maryland is certified to provide stroke care because we shared our story in order to save lives.

I remind my children (now ages twenty-four and twenty-sight)—and they remind me—that our gifts will always open doors to success, and our personal testimonies will always lead us to our purposes in life. My children learned the toughest life lesson far too young, which is the death of a parent. It has continued to transmute their lives in similar ways as it has mine. I have always challenged them, as I have challenged myself before their eyes, to feel and embrace the process with the intention of becoming a person that they and their father would be proud of on the other side of each and every experience. They call me their hero, but they are my heroes. It was the love for and of my children that rescued me from an abyss of despair that would have undoubtedly taken my life whether I continued to breathe or not.

You can call me unstoppable because if my husband's death didn't stop me from pushing forward, nothing will be able to stop me from moving to wherever I'm headed.

GETTING UNSTOPPABLY HEALTHY
Against All Odds

*"Sadly, we women are besieged by breast cancer and other
illnesses or sometimes accidents can change our physical
lives. But these women did not give up. They did what it
took to get healthy and, after they healed, they did what it took to
help other women get healthy. Most of these women didn't
have time for illness and so they got busy living, not
dying. They know the desire to live is stronger than
anything, and they came out healthy both in body and healthier
in spirit. Unstoppable courage and strength."*

~Bershan Shaw

Dr. Nina Savelle-Rocklin

Psychoanalyst and author.
Radio host on losing weight without dieting.

I know a lot about my work because I suffered from weight issues myself. Publicly discussing my eating disorder history on radio shows and other interviews was initially terrifying and took a lot of courage—as did facing breast cancer when I had it. Breast cancer was one of the scariest things I've ever been through, but it also taught me lessons about what's important in life. The most growth comes through the scariest moments of our lives, when we learn what we're capable of and comes to define what's most important.

If people have an issue with me, that's their problem. I've been told several times, "You don't look like a psychoanalyst," which is code for, "You're too young and attractive and female to be a serious analyst; you should be an old guy with a beard!" But comments like that make me even more determined to succeed. I respond, "Well, this is what a psychoanalyst looks like!"

Since neglect, abuse, and trauma marked my childhood, my greatest success is that these traumatic experiences didn't embitter me to the world. I never lost my optimism and hope that I would create a good life for myself, that I could find love and use my mind to make a difference in people's lives. That optimism supersedes all my individual accomplishments.

I never give up. If there's a problem, I find a solution. If I face a challenge, I find a way to meet it. If I set a goal, I meet it. I don't let fear, self-doubt, or anything else get in my way. I believe in myself and I believe where there's a will, there's a way.

Giving birth is something that I can only do as a woman, which was a tremendous experience, but I'm not sure it lifted me up. Succeeding in my dream to help people all over the world heal from eating disorders has lifted me up. Originally my dream was to have a successful clinical practice, but it's expanded into the books I've written, the radio show I host, and the online program I created. I never dreamed of that!

When I look back, I wish I had faced my social anxiety earlier and trusted myself more. But today I am happy. My challenge is to balance work and life. Luckily, I have an amazing husband who works from home, does school drop-off and pick up, does laundry and cooks. I couldn't do what I do without him, but I know I work too much and hope to spend more time with my family. Like go on more vacations and take more figure skating lessons.

I always tell my girls that no matter what they choose to do, give it their best and try their hardest. I tell them not to be afraid of failure, because it's inevitable and they can learn from it. I tell them to be their most genuine and authentic selves and never conform to someone else's idea about who they should be or how they should act.

If I was talking to my twenty-year-old self about the future, I'd say to relax and not be in such a hurry! Achievement is not a race and the beauty of success is all the sweeter for having struggled and overcome challenges. I'd also tell myself to think about what I think of others and to trust my ideas, perceptions, and values instead of worrying so much about what others think of me. I'd tell myself to have more fun and be less self-conscious. And then I'd show her photos of my beautiful children and handsome, accomplished husband and say, "You're going to go through hell. But you have heaven waiting for you on the other side."

Katrina L. Shaw

**From breast cancer survivor to
breast cancer advocate.**

My cancer diagnosis was unbelievable to me. I had no
family history and was healthy, exercised regularly,
and watched what I ate. My husband was my biggest inspiration. A
year prior he was diagnosed with prostate cancer. He reminded me
if God blessed him that He would do the same for me. We were both
blessed that it was caught early and neither of us had to go through
the process of getting chemo or radiation. I trusted God through
the process which gave me the peace, strength, and courage to get
me through. My other brave moment was when my husband and I
spent time with my stillborn daughter after giving birth. That was
such a devastating and hard time. I was only at twenty-two weeks
when my membrane was exposed, then after holding on with my
little girl Mireya for two weeks, my water broke, forcing me into
labor only to give birth to my stillborn child. We spent time with

our daughter to have closure. My other brave moment was when I prayed and asked God for me to make the three-hour drive to be there with my mom when she transitioned.

I developed a complex when I was younger because I would get teased because of my dark skin. It wasn't until I got older that I knew my black skin was beautiful. But before that, I got involved in the wrong relationships. My ex-husband was a drug user and abusive to me mentally and physically. I was in that marriage for seven years and missed opportunities that would have been life changing. But I have learned to be strong, encouraging, empowering and to inspire others to walk in their truth and be authentic. When you go through trials and challenges in life, you look at life differently; I achieved a closer relationship and connection with God from all the pain I have been through. I realized that God made me go through it all so I could overcome and use my story for His glory. God always has the final say. I have learned to train myself to find the blessing in any situation.

I have succeeded in my life dream, and I am looking to do so much more. My dream was to help inspire, encourage, and make life better for someone else—to be able to speak all over the world. I am an author, a brand promoter to help others live a better life through premium nutrition, a blog writer, and now CEO and founder of a nonprofit organization called Mammograms Are Not Enough (MANE). This organization will help with funding for breast cancer screening for those who do not have insurance for extra diagnostic screenings—sonograms, new 3D screens, MRI, and all other medical expenses related to the disease. This organization will also provide educational information on the importance of early detection. There are too many women getting breast cancer every year and too many dying from this disease. I want to be a blessing to others which is my gift and passion. I am looking to take all my dreams to the next level to be an advocate, life and health coach, and motivational speaker.

God has blessed me with a great husband, family, and friends. I have been blessed with several awesome opportunities to be an author, the first with this project, and I am so grateful for Bershan. I am meeting some wonderful new ladies and making great connections.

As a breast cancer survivor, I know I have to always keep up with eating correctly, exercising, and keeping stress levels down, which at times is not easy. You really have to stay focused and trust God when you have a health challenge because if your mindset is not right, you can fall off the deep end just thinking about what could or would happen. There are so many commercials now on television regarding breast other cancers. I just change the channel. I am so grateful for life. I know that in life, even though you can prepare, there will always be unexpected storms that will be hard to endure. We all will endure storms in our lives, and some will be harder than others. God wants us not only to continue to trust Him in the storms but how we go through it all is as important as going through it with trust and authenticity.

Silvana Cusimano
Breast cancer survivor x 2.

*M*y mother and I were not at all prepared for the inevitable. When my dad (eighty-seven years old) went into the hospital on December 7, 2018, he was suffering from a lumbar fracture, making him sedentary at home for over two weeks. When he struggled to walk around the house, I knew he had to go to the hospital. He was also legally blind due to both eyes having a retinal detachment and could not speak English very well. All of this combined stress put my father into delirium and he completely shut down, not eating or drinking, and pulling the IVs out of his arms. I was watching a grown man try to crawl out of his skin. One week later, he was transferred to a nursing rehabilitation home.

Two days later, he went into cardiac arrest soon after I left for an hour; he was rushed back to the hospital where they revived him long enough for me to say goodbye. Walking alone into that emergency room and seeing him lying there like Jesus Christ on the cross, with wires and tubes coming out of his body, not knowing if he was coherent, I held his hand and prayed over him to go peacefully. I prayed he saw his family and that his sight was given back and that he will know how much he was loved and to be happy. Then I walked out of the room and waited for my eighty-six-year-old mother to get to the hospital so she could say goodbye to her husband. This was truly a wake-up call that life is short.

I don't necessarily feel being a woman has held me back. I am who I am and I make no apologies, staying true to being who I am as a woman! In some instances, people assume being attractive gets you in the door, but I believe that confidence is what gets you there. I'm from a background of strong, resilient women. It's my mother I admire the most, always joking with her that she has nine lives like a cat. I look to her for strength and motivation to keep me grounded and keep me going. And, in turn, I try to do the same in being a role model not only to the women in my family, but to my closest friends and their children.

Being an only child, I always dreamt of getting married and having a lot of children. Unfortunately, that did not happen; and for a while I thought that was the end of it. But I realized that marriage and children do not define you. And as it is said, you do not have to give birth to a child to be a mother. I now have two amazing stepsons whom I have influenced and impacted and who have now given us two amazing granddaughters. I believe I am a mother to all the children in my life and inspire them to be the best they can be.

There is so much I would have done differently, including following my dream of performing. When I was in high school, I tried out for a lead role in Grease. I was always in dance, but really wanted to sing. I got the role of Marty. I was so thrilled that I was recognized for my potential singing talent! However, my boyfriend who was two years older than me and very possessive wouldn't let me take the role. I dropped out before I could get started . . . what a mistake! Who knows where I would be today? I also went to an all-girl business school instead of traditional college initially. I would have loved the experience of going away to college and to grow independently without having a boyfriend; sometimes my parents dictated my life.

As I got older and became more confident and wise, the tides changed. Once I made the decision to break away from my boyfriend and started experiencing life, I embraced my independence, which helped me become the woman I am today. I'm grateful that I'm healthy and surrounded by my mom, partner, stepchildren, family near and far, and a wealth of friends who love and emotionally support me.

One of my biggest challenges is getting my career back on track. When I made the decision to go into retail, I went into it with an agenda (in my early thirties). Having no retail experience, I stayed the course, going into a keyholder position ending with a district sales manager position less than three years later. That was one of my biggest accomplishments; being in that role for several years, I kept learning so I could continue to get to the next level.

After going through breast cancer while I was working and then losing my job, it was challenging to look in the mirror and not see me. I didn't see that vivacious outgoing woman I was before cancer and who I became again. I had to change my mindset and get my confidence to get back out there. Since then, I reestablished myself as a retail leader working towards a district sales manager position.

The only thing that was holding me back is me. I know, based on my reputation and experience and the positive impact I have on the people I meet for the first time, that this should speak volumes. I was once described as having a colorful personality. I found that to be funny, but in thinking about it, I think I do. When I meet someone for the first time, I find a way to connect with them or find out how we may be connected, like six degrees of separation. I am not afraid to speak to anyone at any level. I know that retail is not what I am going to be doing for the rest of my life, but it's what I am supposed to being doing right now.

Looking back, I would have been more frugal with my money and would have invested it more wisely so I would have a more comfortable life today. I also believe if I started my career in retail in my twenties, I would have been president of a brand today! My advice to my stepchildren, grandchildren, nieces, and nephews is to follow your passion and your heart. You only have one life to live so make it great. Learn to love yourself and live life to the fullest. Be kind, honest, and happy. No judgement—live and let be! I am currently the store manager of Pandora in Soho on Broadway in New York City.

I see myself possibly writing my own book about connections. I also see myself continuing to make a positive impact on people's lives by inspiring and motivating them. I see myself moving further away from retail and more towards having a platform to be able to help women who are facing challenges. When I received the call from my doctor with my cancer diagnosis, it felt like I was punched in the stomach. I didn't know what to do or how to react. I was stunned. After telling my partner the results, he immediately turned around and said to me, "You cannot change the outcome, and we will face it head on together."

I thought about it for a few minutes and I made my first call to my best friend. As I was talking to her, she started to breakdown, and at that moment I went into survival mode and was the one who comforted her. Then, I made the next call to another best friend and she broke down. I immediately said to her, "I am going to hang up the phone. Call me back after you compose yourself so we can talk." These conversations continued in the same fashion. However, the next morning I had to break the news to my mom, who is also a breast cancer survivor, and she almost fell on the floor. I knew that I had to rise above and stand up to this dreadful disease and realize that I needed to be here for my family and my friends. When I received the outpouring of support from friends that I had not been in contact with for over ten, fifteen, and some twenty years, it showed me what a positive impact I must have had in their lives and that my purpose is to be a positive influence and a role model, not only to them but to their children. The cancer took my fertility, but I have amazing stepsons who have supported me throughout my journey. I am surrounded by all my friends' beautiful children who inspire and motivate me to want to always try to shine a light and look to me for guidance. I believe that life is for the living and we must make the most of what it has to offer us.

Then one day I looked at myself in the mirror and didn't like what I saw. It wasn't me; I had gained over twenty-five pounds, lost my job, and was falling into depression. I knew it was time to make a change. I had to stop making excuses and take charge of my health and my life by regaining my strength and proving to myself I could overcome any obstacles before me. A friend of mine encouraged me to do Tough Mudder with her, an extremely challenging race in which participants have to overcome physical obstacles.

At first, I was reluctant but she convinced me to look at it as an opportunity to overcome the obstacles before us. With that, I started boot camp with a great team of trainers to help prep for the

race and it opened up a whole new world for me. I lost the weight, got in shape, got through the race, as well as opened myself to other races, one of which was SpartanSprint
where I had the opportunity to be part of the CNBC Series to inspire others, especially women.

My motto is, "Don't let cancer get in the way of your life. Let your life get in the way of cancer."

Dr. Missy Johnson
Breaking free: Fearless in the face of cancer.

*T*here have been so many times when I've had to be fear-less. That explains the title of my newest book: *Fearless Faith, Life After Cancer: How to Survive a Life Tsunami and Win* (2018). Just twenty-four hours after I received my life-shattering diagnosis, I was standing to accept the President Barack Obama Lifetime Achievement Award. I had chosen not to tell my family until after I received the award that I had stage 3C breast cancer. I didn't know if I had the strength to keep fighting, but I wanted it to be the greatest moment of my life for the sake of my family.

It seems like if you stay back and stay quiet, you can be OK, but the higher I went into corporate America, the more racism I saw. A lot of people did not know how to receive a Black woman in a high position. It was very challenging and it's certainly one of the reasons that I founded CTC Personal Development Insti-tute, an organization that shows women in corporate America how to redevelop, rebrand, and reposition themselves in order to transition from corporate America to entrepreneurship. I'm a John Maxwell-certified trainer, and in addition to the Lifetime Achievement Award, I have been included in the 2018 *Michigan Chronicle* Women of Excellence.

It has always been my desire to show other women that I never give up and they should never give up, either. I am a fearless fighter and I never let them see me sweat. Being able to bounce back and break free has helped me become an award-winning, number-one best-selling author, speaker, and coach with mastery in personal and leadership development.

That said, I am always a work-in-progress, counting small successes. I dream of showing women that they can restart, rebuild, and rebrand themselves and live in their authentic purpose. I wanted other women to look into and talk about their experiences, so I'm the CEO of Fearless Women Rock LLC, a platform created for women to share their courageous stories so they can leverage themselves to accomplish their professional goals.

I believe happiness is a measurement of many things, but I would say I am free; if that's what happiness is, then I am happy. But I am challenged to stay on task. I meet those tasks on my own, but if I had the right team in place, I wouldn't have to stretch things out until the eleventh hour, and that would relieve some tension. I've been recognized for the work I've done and continue to do. I've been featured in many types of media, including the *Speaker's Magazine*, Power Network Conference, NBC, ABC, *Huffington Post*, and *Marie Claire*, to name a few.

If I could change anything about my life right now, it would be my finances. I'd upgrade my life to have more money if I could. Money is required to build out the projects I have in mind and to connect with influencers. I always tell people to trust the process. Speak the things you want into existence and live like you already have what you need.

Colleen Jolly
Poles apart:
Finding happiness after a life-shattering accident.

My father wanted a boy, not a useless girl who would marry, change her name, and see the end of his Jolly line. I have one vivid memory of him finally paying attention to me from when I was about five or six years old. He was drunk, which wasn't unusual, and he decided to teach me kung fu, a supremely masculine pursuit which he knew nothing about, having never studied martial arts. We sat on the floor of the tiny dining room in our rent-controlled apartment in Queens with our shirts off. He'd pose, biceps flexed and arms up defensively in imitation of the latest Bruce Lee movie, cigarette dangling precariously from his lip, and then I'd mimic.

We left him when I was eight and moved to Florida to live with my mom's family, going from blue-collar working-class to food-stamp-line poor. In those days, it really was a line you stood in for hours to collect the colorful booklets of tear away "stamps" to exchange at grocery stores while furtively hoarding all coin change to buy necessities the stamps wouldn't cover—like toilet paper.

My mom blamed men—all men, really, but mostly my father and her father—for her lot in life. She never got an education because of men. She never got a chance to do the things she wanted to do in life because of men. Things were harder for her because . . . men. In the same breath she'd complain about them, she also craved their attention and validation. From a very young age, this dichotomy of worth and worthless, men and not-men, burned itself into my brain as I searched to understand my role in the world.

I didn't want to be a woman. My mom taught me that women were victims, even if she never intended to. Life happened to women, and even when they did extraordinary things, it didn't seem to change much. But I clearly wasn't a man, either, despite my drunken kung fu lessons. I was too young to fully understand the complexities of gender. One thing I did understand was that I wanted to be successful and happy and adventurous as a human being. I wanted to have all the same chances as someone else regardless of my lot in life; regardless of whether I was rich or poor, male or female.

I didn't know it at the time, but I started on a journey to forge a new path, one that wasn't limited by a binary view of what men should do and what women should or could do. I'd wind up helping people of all genders find their own agency and take control of first their bodies and then their lives through a very unlikely medium.

On March 28, 2001, my life was almost put permanently on hold when I was hit by a truck. My right leg between my ankle and knee was shattered in a Grade IIB open fracture—the second-worst kind, exposing bone and requiring extensive reconstruction including a skin flap grafted from my upper thigh, and later, a bone graft from my hip. First, the doctors wanted to amputate. Then, they told me I'd never walk again, I'd never dance again, and I'd have to leave school to recover. No. I wanted to be the first person in my family to graduate. I'd worked so hard to get to Georgetown. I had a promising internship and a life that was just starting to take shape. I pleaded with doctors to try to do as much as they could to save my leg. When competing health insurance companies left me footing the bill for hundreds of thousands of dollars, I created my own physical therapy program. In the end I had five surgeries, each more painful than the last, and to this day, I am in constant pain. I regularly set off metal detectors from the pins, plates, and staples still holding my leg together.

Women are expected to be perfect. Perfect and silent. Poised and graceful. Smart, but not too smart. Accessible, but not enough to be labeled a whore. Women are held to extreme standards, not just by men, but by other women, too. And so, we all suffer in silence, perpetuating a standard and paradigm that allows for very little deviation from the norm and punishes those that step out of line through subtle social manipulations. We police this pervasive social Panopticon where there are no watchers at the center of our own morality, but since we believe there are, we ourselves supervise and enforce those unspoken rules, ostracizing those that do not comply. We do this through our direct actions and in our media: Photoshopped glossies forever moving perfection out of reach and leading us to believe whatever new pore-reducer will actually change our lives and make us desirable, complete.

Several years after the accident, on a whim I attended a dance class. That dance class led me to another dance class and another, and before I knew it, one night I was standing in the middle of a pole-dancing class surrounded by writhing women in booty shorts, sweating and grinding in a room full of chrome poles. There I was, surrounded by women in very short and colorful shorts, with their cellulite blatantly exposed to the fresh air—and they were laughing.

These women, ranging in age from twenties to sixties, in all shades of the rainbow and in every size, were enjoying their bodies firmly away from the male gaze, dancing under the mood lighting in a nondescript room in a one-story strip mall on a random Tuesday night. They were dancing for themselves and no one else. Enjoying the movement, enjoying their bodies, and the way they responded to the music. Laughing when they tangled themselves up or when sweaty hands made the floor approach a bit too fast. No one looked around self-consciously at mistakes; they just kept moving and laughing.

I was terrible in that first class. The pole studio, as they're called, was small and as we put our jackets on and collected our purses in the tiny room that made up both foyer and dance area, the next class started. The women looked the same, laughing and clad in glittery tank tops and brightly colored shorts, but instead of prancing around the pole, they immediately started to move up it towards the ceiling. Some climbed as if it was a rope in gym class, while others flipped themselves upside down like a scene from a Cirque du Soleil act. I must have been standing with my mouth open for a few minutes before the teacher struck up a conversation. "First day, huh?" she asked conversationally as I nodded, still dumbstruck at the feats of strength being effortlessly performed just feet from where I stood. "These ladies have only been poling for about two months now." She jerked a thumb behind her to confirm we were talking about these extraordinarily normal-looking women and not some other apparitions. As she did, I noticed the muscles in the top of her shoulder move in a way I'd never seen on a woman before.

Hands on her hips now, accentuating a perfect and effortless posture clearly unmarred by years of hunched computer work, she told me, "Come back next week, and soon, that'll be you." She strode purposefully away to the front of class and I found myself nodding. Come back next week? Well, I guess I could. It led to another and another and another. About six months in, I proclaimed to my fiancé that I needed a pole in the house to practice more—I simply wasn't getting strong enough, fast enough. By our wedding a few months later, I maintained a matched set of bruises under each arm from pressing the pole into my bicep to practice inverting my now colorfully clad bottom over my head. Those bruises are visible in every wedding photo where I raised my arms in a most unladylike touchdown position showing how excited and happy I was. I told the photographer not to retouch them.

Within a year, I competed in my first pole-dancing event. Two years later, I opened my own pole studio and just six months after that, I purchased the original event for the pole dance and pole fitness community—the International Pole Convention, or Pole-Con for short—reinvigorating the failing brand and bringing new professionalism and opportunities to almost one thousand annual attendees from all over the world.

It was as if one day I woke up and my whole life had changed. My world used to revolve around work. I doggedly climbed the corporate ladder, dutifully pretending to be "one of the boys" during my partner meetings where I, as the minority partner, only female, and youngest would play secretary because I typed the fastest. I regularly endured countless micro-aggressions from clients and colleagues in the industry for how I dressed and how I wore my hair or the shoes I chose that day—all drably corporate, and sensible pumps with pearl necklaces, of course.

I was in a board meeting once in a mixed group of men and women ranging in age from 30s to 60s, and I disagreed strongly with one of my fellow female board members. I disagreed with her because I thought her approach was wrong and inappropriate for our membership. No one else dared to contradict her on anything, since both her bark and her bite were fierce. We debated professionally for a bit, and I won the rest of the board members over to my side. After the meeting we shared an elevator down to the parking lot, and in a concerned tone she told me how tired I looked. She seemed concerned that I was "getting sick." This fake concern masked her frustration and perhaps perception of losing power to someone else. Regardless of her intent, the action was unnecessary and a thinly veiled way to upset my personal confidence in a professional environment. I had stepped out of my carefully approved role as a younger board member, and I needed to be policed.

These things in my life did not happen in serial order: I only do things in parallel. As I continued my assault on the tiny part of corporate America I was set on dominating, I was, in the evenings, weekends, and every other spare moment in my day, building my knowledge of anatomy and kinesiology; developing an understanding of how aligning your body improves your spirit and mind; and realizing just how healing pole was not just for me but for my growing crop of students.

Through pole, I have gained more compassion. Not just for others but for myself. I no longer look in the mirror and see my flaws first; I see my strengths. I see what I am capable of. When I walk into a room full of my students, whether they are there for the first time or have been with me for years, I don't see their imperfections and I certainly don't see their titles or their pedigrees. I see them emotionally and physically laid bare, raw, dancing practically in their underwear, sweating and grunting and succeeding, surprising themselves by achieving things they never believed were possible and supporting each other while they do it. There is no tearing each other down to perpetuate an outmoded, win-lose system where only one person can succeed while another fails. There are only cheers and sweaty hugs, celebrating all of our successes and literally holding each other up when we feel like we're about to fall.

That feeling of accomplishment, of beating whatever odds you are up against—being "too fat" or "too skinny" or "not good enough" or not "anything" enough—that feeling starts to melt away when you are hanging upside down by your toenail from a slippery metal apparatus and not plummeting to the Earth, firmly thumbing one's nose at the seemingly immutable law of gravity. It's replaced by the feeling that if I can do this, I can do anything!

Maybe my father did get something right after all: there is a strength to strength. Nourishing the physical body can help mend the soul. You can be strong and be a woman, however you define that strength. You can be brave and be a woman. You can be frilly and be a man! You cannot look at someone and know what they are capable of. You cannot measure a person's worth by the size of their biceps or by the size of their bank accounts, and you cannot trace their path through life solely by the lines of their scars.

Every day I get to help women *and* men learn how to live their best lives through the unusual medium of pole dancing. I get to see them grow and flourish, taking the lessons learned in the dimly lit studio back to their real lives and spread that compassion and boundless joy to others. Educating them on self-love, patience, strength, determination, and the limitlessness of the human spirit regardless of its packaging is my passion.

Women don't have the luxury of stopping when they meet obstacles. I've always had to overcome and move past any challenges I've encountered, regardless of people's expectations of what I should or could do, and I am unstoppable!

Celeste M. Mumford
Peace in the storm.

My mother was beautiful and vibrant. She was college-educated, she ran a business, and she seemed to love life . . . and she had health insurance! To this day, no explanation could help me understand why she let breast cancer eat her from the inside out, or why she chose – in my opinion – death. My mother chose to do nothing until it seemed to be too late; the stage 4 cancer was inoperable, so she started with chemotherapy. She helped a friend to navigate her way through a breast cancer diagnosis while remaining silent about hers. I was very angry with my mother's decision—or lack thereof. My mother took her last breath on March 12, 2002, when she was fifty-five. We buried her less than two years after her first doctor's visit. Her friend is still alive.

Following my mother's diagnosis in 2001, I had mammograms every year. I happily received my rose from the women's center after each mammogram and was glad to hear that no cancerous growths were found in my dense breast tissue. Having a clean bill of health year after year made me happy and provided me with reassurance: I feared breast cancer. I've always had a challenging relationship with my breasts. They were too small, too flat, and I really didn't like them much. I entertained the idea of getting implants. I thought implants would help me to love my breasts.

Fast forward to January 2013. Something seemed off. There was no pain or anything, but something just wasn't quite right. I talked myself into believing that my breasts were fine because I had just had a mammogram and annual exam a few months earlier and received another clean bill of health. I was in the habit of performing breasts exams on myself in every way possible: in the shower, standing up, lying down, with hands on my hips, using the breast self-detection kit, hands behind my head, even while standing on one foot. Sometimes I thought I felt something. Other times I didn't feel anything at all.

My mind was racing. I was consumed with thoughts of my mother suspecting that malignant cells were mutating in her body without asking for help or seeking medical attention. These thoughts prompted me to take action. I called my doctor to schedule an appointment. The next available time was March 12—the anniversary of my mother's death twelve years earlier, and nearly two months away. I waited those two months so that I could see the doctor under whose care I'd been for the last few years, but I don't condone waiting that long: early detection can be a life saver!

After what seemed like the longest wait ever, it was finally the day of my appointment. I told the doctor that I felt a lump in my breast. She examined my breast and felt it, too. Neither of us had felt it at any of my earlier appointments. From that moment on, everything moved extremely quickly. Before leaving her office,

I had made an appointment at the Breast Center for the following day. At that appointment, they did a mammogram which showed absolutely nothing! But I had an ultrasound that showed the lump. How could this be?

I was scheduled to see the best breast surgeon in town, who was no-nonsense and to-the-point. She showed me the ultrasound and explained that she believed I had a form of breast cancer. She prepared me for the worst-case scenario; we talked about surgery, chemo, and radiation. First, I had to have a biopsy. About three days later, I was in my car before work when I got the call: the biopsy came back positive for a malignancy. I took a deep breath. The first thing out of my mouth was, "I am not my mother! I am not my mother! I AM more than a conqueror. This disease will not overtake me, nor will I succumb to it."

I met with the breast surgeon after the biopsy to discuss my options. Based on the results, she recommended a lumpectomy and radiation. Heck-to-the-no! I did not want a lumpectomy or radiation. I asked to have a bilateral mastectomy; the doctor thought it was too radical and said she couldn't recommend it due to insurance restrictions. "I know you don't recommend it, but it's what I need . . . can you make it happen?" She said yes, and she did, but I had to actively participate and make choices when it came to my health and course of treatment. I acknowledged my situation and took ownership of my own well-being. I had the bilateral mastectomy; radiation was not recommended.

It took a bit of wordsmithery to advocate for myself, especially when meeting with my breast surgeon. She kept referring to the malignancy as "your breast cancer." I finally corrected her.

"That breast cancer is not mine. There is a malignant lump in my breast, and I'd prefer that you say 'the malignant lump in your breast.'" While the lump was there, it was there illegally and was a foreign entity that had to be destroyed! From that moment on, the surgeon referred to it as "the malignant lump in your breast" instead. My prayer is that she will continue to use that wording with all of her future patients. People too often claim diseases as their own, and it becomes difficult for them to annihilate something they consider a part of them. We claim our children, our marriages, our homes; a breast cancer diagnosis doesn't fit the category.

I had a Job 3:25 experience: For the thing which I greatly feared is come upon me, and that which I was afraid of is come unto me. I had truly feared breast cancer, but here I was, facing it as a reality. God revealed Himself to me in a breast malignancy. The lump didn't miraculously disappear like they sometimes do in church shows, nor did the lump shrink. I, however, already believed that I was healed, even though the malignancy was still growing in my body. There was no supernatural disappearing of the malignancy, so I buckled up for a ride, knowing that God was taking me on the scenic route. I remembered God telling me that I shall live and not die and that my faith had made me whole. This gave me comfort and fortified my belief. Although I would have to endure an arduous process, I could endure it from a place of rest in God. I clung to the Word of God, found peace, and immediately ran to the eye of the hurricane: Christ!

Giving birth to my daughter and raising her to be an independent thinker has been a very uplifting experience. Feminine energy is amazing, and women, by nature, are fierce. I am teaching my daughter and granddaughters not to make permanent decisions based on temporary circumstances. I'm helping them to trust their instincts and to be fearless. I also encourage them to believe they are who God says they are, to trust that God has a plan for them, and to have hope for the future. To walk in love and compassion; to be generous and laugh often.

The sun shines on the just and the unjust, and I know that as long as I am still wearing an earth suit, I will be vulnerable to tribulation, including malignancy. Many of you read the Scripture but are extremely shocked and clutch your pearls when things happen, immediately turning to panic, fear, and insecurity. You question God and stress yourself out over the whys and hows of life. Then you seek the opinions of some of your friends, who like Job's friends tell you how you brought this upon yourself, reminding you of your past sin and more. Some, not knowing any better, will tell you of everyone they've ever heard of who had breast cancer and died.

Participating in the process doesn't mean you necessarily have to agree with what's happening.

It means you are not going to react from an emotional place or from your flesh, but choose to respond from a place of wisdom, self-care, and good information. Many of us immediately tap into our humanity and say, "I'm only human," which isn't true! God wants you to tap into your Divinity and be led by your Spirit! I know this is radical, but I've never looked behind me. When I felt the lump, I only looked forward and up. There's a message in that for somebody. What you focus on grows with you, so don't focus on things behind you—set your sights on things above.

You can call me unstoppable because I refuse to be a victim. I choose to be victorious and empowered. I made proactive decisions when the cancer came by selecting a medical team (oncologist, breast surgeon, and reconstructive surgeon) with whom I was comfortable; I got second opinions and I made informed decisions. I chose to get a bilateral mastectomy. When it came time to decide whether or not to get chemo, I was challenged. From what I'd heard about chemotherapy, I knew I didn't want it.

"You were so radical and bold when you chose a bilateral mastectomy over my recommendation, but now you're getting all soft when it comes to chemo," my surgeon said. She advised that chemo should be part of my plan to do what I can to prevent a reoccurrence. I chose chemo. Some choose not to get chemo. When it came to how I was going to walk in this situation, I chose to believe that God was working all things together for my good. I am unstoppable.

Carol Boardman-Scruse
Lost over 100 lbs.
Found herself.

I found out a few years ago that I was involved in a scam to promote scar creams. Innocently involved, I suffered the loss of my reputation and the possibility of prosecution, not to mention that it took years to be vindicated. It went like this: I was to promote the cream and receive commissions for having my doctor fill out a prescription, have my insurance cover it, and I'd pay the co-pay. If I told other people at my job about the cream as I was promoting it because I was using it, they would get a commission if their doctor approved its use.

Two years later, I got a letter from the attorney general that we were involved in something illegal. Everyone else got the same letter. How could that be? We all got the 1099 form and paid taxes. Everything was written and done via email, text, or phone. How would I think anything was illegal?

Fast forward two more years to September 2018, where the case received publicity. I was put on administrative leave from the job where I had been employed for twenty-five years, working for the State of Connecticut. In all those years, there had never been a disciplinary action against me. I had perfect service ratings and was very well liked. Suddenly I had people hearing all of this crazy stuff about me. I have never in my life done or have been involved in anything illegal. People were calling me and my family. My name was surrounded in negativity. All I could do was cry and try to clear my name.

I had to hire lawyers with money I didn't have. I prayed my name would get cleared in the civil litigation of any criminal wrongdoing. I held my head high, got a part-time job, continued going to the gym, and cried. I couldn't understand how I missed that. I pride myself on being smart, but this I never saw coming. Finally, cleared of any wrongdoing, I went back to work March 1, 2019, with no disciplinary action taken and the case closed. I still have my attorney working on the pieces. But cleared or not, my name was slandered and my character was assassinated. That changed me from so cheerfully trying to help everyone and believe in everyone.

Now I question everyone and everything. I will not ever get involved in anything or put myself in that predicament again. I learned a lot about myself, like how I'm too trusting. I had always talked up and promoted a lot of things for people—my trainers, jewelry, food, oils, my hairdresser, and so on. I learned who was really in my corner in my time of need. And I say that those who really know me knew I would never do anything like that and those are the ones who stayed and are still there.

Yes, being a woman has held me back in a lot of areas. I haven't tried for promotions or certain jobs feeling I wouldn't get them. I have been overlooked for positions. Being a woman has lifted me up because I am a nurturer, I take care of everyone, want to feed everyone, make sure everyone is OK. I want to be there and support my friends and even people with whom I'm really not attached—I want to make sure everyone is OK. I now work with individuals with disabilities. I am a strong advocate for them and their feelings. I am powerful and stand by my decisions.

As a woman I have overcome the odds. My mother throwing me out of the house when I was pregnant made me anxious for security. I had no help from my family or anyone else after I was thrown out of home. Alone and pregnant, I just pushed myself and kept going. I did not give up. I ended up working three jobs while I went to school full-time, first earning my Associates then BHS then M.Ed. degrees. I secured great employment and purchased my home and raised my daughter to be a strong young lady. I have proven to myself that I'm a very strong warrior woman.

My life's dream was to be successful. I have a good career, but this is not my dream of long ago. As many people do, I took my job years ago for security, but my dream isn't to do what I'm doing for the rest of my life. I now want to pursue speaking and coaching people. I want to be in my dream of helping people.

If I could turn back time, I would take risks, accept challenges, do what I wanted to do, and step out of the box. I would have pushed myself to become that great speaker and become visible and known for helping others achieve their goals. I would have pushed and not been scared that if having my own business and becoming successful didn't work out, concerned that maybe my daughter and I would be homeless. That's why I stayed – for comfort and stability. Now looking back, I would have done what I wanted to do and stepped out on faith. And if I fell, I would have gotten back up.

Right now, I feel like I'm just maintaining my day-to-day life, waiting for my pension. Then I can pursue what I want and stop living in a rut. I'll get to be "really happy." My challenges are that I'm the bread winner; it's a comfort zone that I must and will get out of. I need to build confidence, do more speaking, get my words down on paper for my book.

I would advise people not to settle. Way back when, I weighed 300 pounds and was so grateful that anybody would want me that I married my daughter's father. I love my daughter and having her is what motivated me to go back to school and make something of my life. I shouldn't have settled but instead gone on to pursue my dream. I started going to the gym, working out, and over time lost over 130 pounds. That's a pretty good boost to your self-esteem.

Children sometimes don't listen to advice. I told my daughter not to have a baby with someone who was not going to be there in the long run. She did, and now I have a grandson whom I love and wouldn't trade for the world. He didn't ask to be here. There is nothing I would not do for my daughter and grandson or I'd die trying. My advice to her now is: Don't let any man or anyone hold you back from what you want to do. Don't be scared, as I was, and give up your dream. Bring yourself and your son to the highest. My daughter is graduating with her master's degree in counseling and is looking forward to opening her own practice once she's licensed. I told her the world is hers; if she wants it, she has to go get it. Nothing is going to come to her.

All of the trials and tribulations I have been through and overcome have made me strong, self-confident, and an independent warrior woman. I won't stop. I will continue to push through until I get what I want and start a new chapter in my life . . . I am an unstoppable warrior woman!

CHOOSING UNSTOPPABLE
Happiness

*"You'll hear a lot of women talk about happiness being a choice.
It often requires change, getting rid of what is not working,
and that takes big strength and belief in the future.
These women have it. They took risks, did new things, no matter how
old they were, and they arrived at new places that made them happy.
To get somewhere new, you have to choose your happiness and say yes
to it. These women show us how."*

~Bershan Shaw

J. Murphy Lewis

Fashion maven, publisher, philanthropist to Parisian writer.

*W*ho knew I would live my dream of writing and being married to a wonderful man in Paris? It all began by my walking out of a safe career in fashion in New York City as a vice president of international sales for Badgley Mischka to launch a 501c3 Global Voice Foundation. It was started to help the Maasai warriors and the Kalahari San bushmen whom I had been visiting over the course of ten years (seventeen journeys in total). I knew that those experiences in the Kalahari Desert around the fire and in the water and naming ceremonies of my initiation in Kenya had transformed me, giving me the courage to be myself in the world, to live a life as my true self.

I used to feel I was not worthy—feeling I was "the Second Sex," as in the similarly titled book by Simone de Beauvoir, that there was something wrong with me, that I was less than a man.

But being a woman has given me the right to feel, to sense into myself through psychology, and to listen to the nightscape of dreams. And therefore, this in the end serves me to listen to those inner landscapes, exploring and venturing into them as a way into who I was meant to be and through whom I have become.

I am now succeeding in my dreams by "writing for my life," married and living with an incredible man in Paris, and serving through Global Voice Foundation and sharing with others in a loving environment through the Akashic Records, which are a type of database of what will happen, is happening, or has happened as believed by those who follow holisticism.

I wouldn't change a thing in my life. I feel that each step, each experience, has served me and developed me into who I am to this day. From time to time, I remind my child within: "All along—we, you, and I, little Irene, have had a guiding self within and therefore have been living our life on purpose." I am thoroughly happy. And when I'm not, when something rears its head, I know there is something more to explore into and through. I go back down and into that, so I can thread that experience in this life or in a past life so it becomes part of the greater tapestry of my "I am" self.

My biggest challenge now is editing a three-book memoir and letting it go into the world. If I could change anything about my life it would be to trust the process more and to know the wound is sacred and is part of what I have to offer. To understand when I'm struggling through something of the past that made me feel as though I was "hurt"—that this struggle is only to inform me how it felt at the time in order that I can compassionately understand others, as well as myself, and so I can explain this to my readers and to those I work with in the Akasha. That in fact,

I'm not "that"—a wounded human being or a victim—that I am instead a soul choosing this body and this experience at this time to live here on this planet. I am greater than all of those experiences combined, and no one has the power to crush my soul.

I would advise all children that you, my darlings, have something to offer to the world that no one else does—that's why you're here!

Ann M. Rothschild

**Seminar leader,
Therapist, who brought happiness to herself.**

ot everybody decides to leave their marriage of forty-one years (relationship of fifty years) at the age of seventy But I did. It was my best moment. I've been lifted up during it all by amazing women friends, by amazing men who have loved me, and with more credit than I deserve for my athletic prowess, especially my extreme skiing. I'm in the process of surpassing life dreams. I've found more love than I could have ever imagined. I'm also writing a book, another thing I couldn't even dream.

If I could change anything, I would have taken myself and my education more seriously. I would have spent more time with myself and my kids by easing up my ambitions. I would have held out for way more before and during my marriage. I'm still insecure and have many moments of fear, worry, struggle, and sadness. But overall, I'm often very happy. Many days it bubbles up hourly.

Getting a divorce is bigger and harder than I imagined. Wrenching myself out of a life I worked to build for fifty years is hugely challenging. I'm fully upended and out on a limb in my seventies. My two sons have mixed allegiances and I'm having to confront fears and the big risks I'm taking. That said, I'm in the process of making my life more financially secure. I didn't pay attention because, so far, I've lived only as a daughter and a wife. I was negligent and irresponsible in turning my life over to others. I want to change that now and take full responsibility for all facets of my life but particularly my finances.

I'm encouraging my married son to partner with his wife. I've advised him to share his fears as well as his finances. I'm advising my younger son to take more risks and not settle for a relationship that is anything less than the love of his life.

Elisabeth Amaral

**Writer and successful real estate woman.
Always true to herself.**

I have taken many actions that required courage in order to get through the day because I have a strong survival instinct. I would say that my most courageous act was to divorce my second husband in order to maintain my sanity, but I am not brave. I have never let anything hold me back because of the fact that I am a woman and never paid any attention to anyone who ever tried. Motherhood is the part of womanhood that has lifted me up.

My dream, my determination, was to experience life on my terms. I did, but often at a steep price to myself and others. I did what I wanted to do and achieved more than I thought I would, despite the obstacles I placed in the way of what I assume was my search for happiness. I now have a life that I cherish, made richer by the hard times. It's my history. It astounds me when I recall all that I've experienced. It feeds my stories.

That said, I wish I'd taken myself more seriously as a writer at a much earlier age. I had the chance to go to law school, but I made up ridiculous reasons not to go. I wouldn't have practiced but that knowledge carries a lot of protection. Speaking for the present, I would like to be more disciplined with my writing and kinder and more understanding to those in need, or to those who move to a different rhythm.

That said, I am content and fulfilled. Finally. It took decades, with long periods of intense anguish and insecurity. I have a solid marriage, a son with whom I have a close relationship, and a granddaughter who redefines the meaning of love. I've managed to write the books I needed to write, at least so far. So yes, I'm happy in a non-gleeful way. I survived a lot of problems to get here. My main challenge is to stay strong and healthy. I had a heart attack over five years ago. I had no pain, just an odd, constant heat in my upper left arm so I waited almost too long before going to the hospital. I had for the most part lived my life based on instant gratification, so it's not been easy taking care of myself in the way I must.

My son is grown and has a young daughter. I give him advice all the time, about everything. He usually doesn't need or want it but he must have listened to me over the years because he has grown into a kind person who does his fair share. For specific advice, I give this to him and to anyone else who's interested: Never, ever have anyone in your life who is not nurturing, who makes you feel negative about yourself, or mistreats you. I would suggest ceasing such a relationship immediately. All it should take, basically, is a heartfelt "See you later," unless the recipient of your words is deranged on some level. Then run. I'm not kidding. Trust your instincts and your dreams. Don't let anyone take them away, ever.

Cee Cee Caldwell
Woman of grace, opulence and destiny.

I came into this world prematurely, weighing just four pounds, two ounces, born to a single mother with three children to raise and support; and she did just that. She was sick all of my life, so my role with her, my favorite person on the planet, was different than most. She worked to support us all and then when she came home, she was so exhausted all she could do was rest. It became my responsibility to be the surrogate mom to my brothers and take on all my mother's normal responsibilities— cooking, cleaning, doing laundry, and everything else that needed to be done to ease my mom's load. I had two big brothers but, for the typical reasons, the responsibility for everything in the home became mine. I didn't ask for it, nobody asked me if I wanted to do it. I simply had no choice but to assume this adult role. Having to take on the role of a caretaker was hard and heavy, so much so that I started drinking even before I was legally allowed to. I did anything I could to chase away the pain I was feeling.

Using alcohol and seeking love is not a good combination. As I was taking care of my mom and brothers, going to school, and being loved (so I thought), I was feeling empty inside. I kept trying to fill the void with unhealthy things. I had to grow up faster than I wanted but this was just the beginning of what life had in store for me.

I have had many brave, profound moments but perhaps trying to continue living after being raped by a member of my church in my own home tops the list. I was just sixteen years old. He came upstairs with a knife, raped me, and went back downstairs as if nothing had happened. I immediately called one of my best friends and told him. While the rapist was still in the house, I raced to my friend. We called my mother and then the police came; I was sent to the emergency room, only to be violated again by going through the dreaded rape kit while being asked a bunch of questions.

It got worse. My mother told me not to press charges. I was completely stunned. I had just experienced the most horrific experience of my life and this is what I am told by the woman who birthed me? I was absolutely devastated. I became angry, bitter, hurt, and wanted to drown the pain in any way I could. I became rebellious. I drank more to numb my feelings and escape a world that seemed to care so little for me. I cared so little for me.

After searching and searching to find love, I finally found it. I met an amazing human being who showed me the love, affection, and attention for which I was looking. Our relationship was a whirlwind, we dated, got engaged, and married within six months. I became a pastor's wife. I thought it was a Cinderella story and I thought that my prayers were answered. I loved him and he loved me, as far as I knew. He made me laugh and we enjoyed each other. But not long after we were married, his children came to live with us and that was another role that was added to my suitcase: stepmother.

So I was then a wife and a stepmother, and I had to deal with baby-mama drama and everything in between. I began to drown in the pool of ministry. As the years went by, I felt like I was no longer a priority in his life and that the job, the church, the children, and quite frankly everyone and everything else was more important than me. I became isolated and depressed. Whatever I was told, I believed and it simply was what it was. I did everything I thought was required of me. As the marriage continued, I felt more and more alone but I continued to fight because "what God joined together let no man put asunder."

I prayed to God for my husband and for me, but received no answer to the pain and hurt I was feeling inside. I cried out to God, "Why is this happening, what did I do to deserve this?" The silence was deafening. I continued to fall deeper and deeper into a hole of depression and no one in my life seemed to know. I was a great actress and I should have gotten an Oscar for the performance of a lifetime. People saw what I allowed them to see. I realized after long contemplation, introspection, and reflection that I married a male version of my mother and that I was not his wife, I was his third child. I had to make the hardest decision in my life: I had to choose me without feeling guilty, a failure, or selfish. After suffering some of the most painful things in my life, I finally allowed myself to look myself in the mirror and tell myself the truth. I had lost my identity and forgotten who God made me to be in an effort to please everyone else but God and me. I knew the gifts, talents, and abilities I had but somewhere in the marrying and caretaking, I had forgotten about my wants, needs, and desires. I really just forgot how to be me.

Being a woman has held me back in a few ways. Because of what happened to me at sixteen, I was made to feel unworthy and not enough. My self-esteem at times has been at rock bottom. I felt inferior to men and have felt as if I had to dumb down so that I would be accepted and loved by them. I have taken so much nonsense from men over the years thinking it was love and it was not. Frankly, I did not love myself or know myself so it could not have been love, it was convenience. I thought that being a woman at times was a curse; I have been mistreated, disrespected, used, and abused. And I allowed it. I take full responsibility for giving up my power to them so that they could make me feel devalued and powerless.

Yet being a woman has lifted me up in so many ways. Once I realized that God created me as a woman of grace, opulence, and destiny with a purpose on this earth to pursue, I changed how I looked at myself and what I allowed others to do to me. I began to stand up for myself and realize how powerful, fearless, amazing, and smart I am. I had the example of a single mother who was a survivor of so many issues and challenges in her own life. I was given birth by a warrior, a champion, and an unstoppable woman. I was taught to be strong, resilient, and determined to be all that God fearfully and wonderfully made me be, no matter what. As a woman, I know that I was made to do some remarkable things in this world and that no matter how long it takes, I will accomplish everything that I desire to achieve in this life.

I have yet to accomplish my soul's purpose, but I am on my way. Since I was a little girl, I dreamed of being a significant serving soul, helping people transform their lives. I had to go through some things in my own life that would prepare me to share my testimony with others of how I made it through. I am a work in progress, but I will manifest this dream and the other dreams that have been resting quietly in my soul. I was born a dreamer and my dreams are BIG and they can't be accomplished by myself. I know that when the appointed time comes, I will be soaring to new heights and helping others realize their dreams too.

I wish I had chosen me first and learned to see my worth and my value much sooner than I did. I have always put other people's needs and wants before my own. I would make better choices and assess the cost before just jumping into things like relationships, businesses, and so much more. I would honor myself by teaching others how to treat me. I would set boundaries that were uncrossable even if I had to walk my journey by myself. I am happy because my happiness is not predicated on people, money, places, or things, it is connected to my allegiance to Jesus Christ. I have learned that happiness is a choice; I choose not to allow the outside to infiltrate my inner happiness.

My biggest challenge right now is starting my life over and being confident that I can do it. Just the thought of having to begin again is paralyzing and scary. I have started businesses, lost businesses; lost money, friends, family, and dreams; and more important than any of that, I have lost me. I am on a renewed search for the real me, the woman who I was designed to be. I have so many role models, but just to name a few: my mother, of course, the conquering life-giver; Dr. Maya Angelou, a word master; Velma Speakman, a powerful Woman of God; and every woman who once was silent and now stands up and fights for what is right for her and lives her own life with intensity and passion.

What I see for my future is absolutely breathtaking. I see a future full of love, light, and colorful experiences that not only change my life but the world around me as well. I will walk tall, stand strong, speak life and live, laugh, love and dance like nobody's watching. And even if they are, I will do it all my way with grace, dignity, integrity, and favor.

I am an Unstoppable Warrior Woman because I am a designer's original, armed for battle, ready to defeat my enemies and my inner me, if necessary. I am me. I don't quit. I reevaluate and then I move forward with vigor, zest, and exuberance. I am a solution looking for a problem to solve that will transform this world into a better place because I was here. I am unstoppable and I am a difference-maker.

Linda Susan Husser

Be bold, beautiful, brand new.

*B*ecause I have been a hairstylist and salon owner for twenty-nine years, I didn't have the same hurdles to face as other women may have. Being a business owner and controlling my own destiny by my work ethic and professionalism put me in control and therefore I was able to blaze my own trail.

Being a woman has lifted me up because I believe God gave us the gift of compassion and empathy. This doesn't mean that men can't be, but part of being a woman is that softer side that we can exhibit without fear of being perceived as weak. I am also lifted up as I see the dramatic changes that women are making in the world with the "Me Too" movement, Woman's March, and the role we are playing in the political process. In the words of the Chaka Khan and Whitney Houston, "I'm every woman, it's all in me!"

My dream has evolved as I have. As a child I thought I wanted to be a lawyer and an actress. I say "think" because how many of us really know what we want to be? I am sure some people do; however, I personally believe most of us are just trying to find our way. Or we are what our parents say we are. One thing I can say is that using my voice has always been an important constant in my life. I have always been a great communicator. That's why it's no surprise to me that I am the Bodacious Lifestyle Coach now and help Black women over forty regain their spark, reclaim their power, and rock their radiance!

I'm called the "SHAME Changer," because I founded the African American Herpes Alliance in 2016. The idea is to change the game of shame for anyone ready, willing, and able to live free from its shackles. Through my own self-development work, I was able to own and release the shame I secretly carried for thirteen years. The SHAME acronym describes the aspects that keep us bound: secrets, hurts, anger, mindset, and emotions.

While my shame point was herpes, my purpose is to assist others in identifying their own points of shame and find a place of surrender and self-love. I want to empower as many people as possible to release their shackles, regain their self-esteem, and step out of the shadows to reclaim their power and share their stories. I hope the need to be free will grow greater than the chokehold that shame has over our minds, bodies, and spirits so that we can live bold, brave, and brand new! By using my voice, I am able to encourage those I work with to make midlife their best life and create the bodacious lives they desire and deserve.

Given the chance, I would have worked on overcoming my fears and falling in love with myself earlier in life. Caring about what people thought about me wouldn't have been such a big deal either. Now, I truly understand that I am not what has happened to me and I get to choose who I am and not be defined by my past.

Once I picked up the pen and started to write brand-new chapters of my life, I could create a new story. It is very uplifting to be able to reinvent myself and step out of the shadows, stop playing small, and stand in my phenomenal power.

The challenge I face right now is technology. I am getting my coaching practice going and because I have been primarily doing hair for more than half of my life, I am not as well-versed as some may be with websites, social media, apps, and how best to use these ways of communicating. Honestly, I wouldn't change a thing about my life. There was a time when I thought it would be cool to erase all the misery and pain that I have felt. But that would also erase the life lessons I have learned and the people that helped me have breakthroughs. My life hasn't been all trials and tragedies either. I have had many good days. I am glad that I was able to weather my storms in life because now I get to help others weather theirs, as well. Honestly, the older I get, I am starting to figure out this thing called life. It definitely has some twists and turns, but I just get in the car of life, strap myself in, and enjoy the ride! I don't have children but I know that if I did I would tell them that life isn't always going to give them what they want, but to stay flexible, focused, and fearless.

I'm an unstoppable warrior woman because I stepped past that "never let them see you sweat!" admonition. Translation: Fake the funk and mask your true feelings, if need be. However, this sets us up for emotional failure. In the SHAME Free Zone, vulnerability and transparency are the two emotional wrecking balls used to destroy shame. I tell everyone what I live by; get out of the prison shame. No magic fairy dust or wands can do the trick. You have to do the work the old-fashioned way! But you will be so much stronger, confident, and proud that you were able to slay the dragon that has held you in bondage for so long. Find a place of surrender and self-love. People will continue to hurt us as long as we live, but we can still choose to keep our eyes toward all that is light, joyful, and clean. That's what makes us all unstoppable.

Natalie Wanner
Having the Courage to Create her own Version of Marriage.

I was born and raised in Sudbury, Ontario, Canada, and now live in Spruce Grove, Alberta, Canada. I am forty-one years old. Being a woman always seemed to mean being the "other" to the male. It meant that if I did what I wanted, like opening my marriage which I did in my late 30s, that I wouldn't have the same accolades as the male. I wouldn't be celebrated for acknowledging my sexuality and in fact I would be ostracized for not being "ladylike" or worse, a "whore," terms I have never truly understood. Growing up there was always a script for the woman, a way to be, to behave, and act. All of those things meant I shouldn't live freely but instead be bound to a box of what a woman "should" be. At some point you have to believe you are more than your gender, more than a made-up script, and more than the ideas of others.

That's when I knew that being a woman was my strength, the day I realized that it was all a lie. Just because there is some outdated, made-up recipe for women to follow doesn't mean anything. Women are the underdogs; we have been since the beginning so it offers me great comfort, pride, and confidence that they never see us coming.

It took nearly thirty-five years to get brave enough, to be fed up enough to live for what I want, regardless of how that "looks" as a woman. Three weeks a month I live in Western Canada where I drive carpool, volunteer at my daughter's school, and make dinner for my husband and children. The other week I live as a single woman in Manhattan. New York has always been a large part of my dream; I made my dream whole once I decided I was good enough to write and then I became a writer in New York. It was a dream I believed was dead, gone, and buried until I decided that my dreams still have to matter and that it's OK to be more than just a wife and mother. I could be me.

It took me a long time to get there. Before I was honest about the life I wanted to live, I caused a lot of hurt, told a lot of lies, and wasted a lot of time making excuses for my desire to be polyamorous. I would have loved to start living my life sooner but I'm grateful I started at all. I don't know that I have ever been happier in my life, living this openly and freely. I find my bouts with anxiety and depression have all but vanished. There's a peaceful feeling when you step into your life and feel confident that it's right for you and then what others think or say can't touch you or hold you down. That is the most powerful feeling I have ever experienced.

Currently, my biggest challenge is making sure that I am the best role model for my daughter. It's constantly trying to find or fake confidence and courage to deal with life's situations appropriately, knowing that she looks to me for guidance. It's being a strong woman, even if I don't feel like one that day and it's making sure that her opinion means more to her than anyone else's. It's making sure she knows her worth and instilling in her a quiet strength that others cannot touch or destroy. I've been faking my confidence for so long I should just have it by now.

There are some things in my life I would tweak like the area I live or the amount of time I get to spend in my single life in New York. Overall, I'm in a place where I feel extraordinarily proud of where I took my dream and the journey I took to get here. I have a twenty-one-year-old son and a seven-year-old daughter, and the one thing I try to teach them is that their lives are theirs and they can spend them however they want . . . just make sure you spend the way you dream about. Chase your happiness and be unapologetic in it.

Bershan Shaw's
Four Steps to
Mindset Freedom

Change your Viewpoint.

*A*s hard as it seems to change what has happened to you, it is necessary in order to break free from the chains that are holding you back. Everything in life happens for a reason. It is for you to grow, help others, learn who you don't need in your life or what you don't want in your life, or to be a teacher and a support system for others. Your journey of heartache experiences is bigger than you.

Getting stage 4 breast cancer was the most horrific experience I ever could have imagined but I had to realize that it was bigger than me. I know I have helped millions around the world through my podcast "Buckle Up with Bershan," my online Warrior Training International, and speaking on stage around the world. I know it sounds strange but cancer was my gift. You too should find the purpose in your pain and that too will push you forward to freedom.

Stop Running Away from Your Past.

Accept and understand that it was and is your past. You can't change it. You can't hide it and you can't run from it. All of those things will leave you balled up with anger, depression, anxiety, and hurt. Instead of trying to avoid it, embrace it. I know it's hard to do. I know that it hurts to think you may have to embrace a rape or a horrible marriage with domestic violence and verbal abuse. I know it may hurt to think about the day when someone broke into your home. But in order to move past those "ugly issues," you must embrace that it happened. You must acknowledge that it happened so that you can scream and yell about it with a therapist or a coach and then move forward.

Stop Blaming and Start Forgiving.

Stop playing the blame game in your heart and recycling the hate. Yes, someone was responsible for the wrongdoing and yes, it made you feel bad. But in order to be set free, you have to stop telling the blame story over and over again because it keeps you stuck. It's time to be free and the only way you can be free is to let go and forgive. It's very hard to forgive someone who did something harmful to you, but we are all human and many of us don't have the tools to do right. They too were victims and they got treated horribly and just recycled the bad behavior. It's time to be the bigger person so the anger won't stay within; forgive so that you can let go.

Let Go.

Letting go is the last step to your freedom. You can never forget but you must move past the hate and the horror of the events in order to let go. Learn the lesson. Use it as a springboard to teach others. Know that you were meant to grow and share your story with others so you can help them. Letting go of the hurt, the pain, and the event will help you become free so you can move ahead with your life. You will never forget, but you will start a new chapter in your life that will be bigger, better, and more productive on your terms.

Acknowledgments

I would like to thank all the women who helped me with this book. All of the women who are in this book. All of the women who gathered stories, found amazing women to get this book published.

We are all warriors. You know who you are. We are in this together. We fight. We make mistakes. We get it wrong. We fail but no matter what we get back up because we are all Unstoppable Warrior Women and there is nothing that can stop us. I just want to thank you all for believing in this movement.

About the Author

$\mathcal{B}$ershan Shaw is a TV personality, global Motivational Speaker, Business & Career Executive Coach, Strategist and a Diversity & Inclusion Trainer. Bershan is the CEO of Warrior Training International (WTI), which helps companies for over 13 yrs with Interactive Training solutions from employee motivation to Senior leadership workshops to career & executive coaching.

"I will take you from where you are to where you want to be"
Bershan Shaw CEO of Warrior Training Int'l
Executive Leadership Trainer Public Speaker Trainer Business & Leadership Strategist Diversity & Inclusion Expert

9 781642 799156